AF386416

THE SILENT WAR

THE SILENT WAR

A PRIVATE MILITARY CONTRACTOR'S MEMOIR FROM EDINBURGH TO BAGHDAD

SCOTT WHITE

Pen & Sword

MILITARY

AN IMPRINT OF PEN & SWORD BOOKS LTD.
YORKSHIRE – PHILADELPHIA

First published in Great Britain in 2026 by
PEN AND SWORD MILITARY
An imprint of
Pen & Sword Books Limited
Yorkshire – Philadelphia

Copyright © Scott White, 2026

ISBN 978 1 03618 029 4

The right of Scott White to be identified as the Author of this work has been asserted by him in accordance with the Copyright, Designs and Patents Act 1988.

A CIP catalogue record for this book is available from the British Library.

All rights reserved. No part of this book may be reproduced, transmitted, downloaded, decompiled or reverse engineered in any form or by any means, electronic or mechanical including photocopying, recording or by any information storage and retrieval system, without permission from the Publisher in writing. NO AI TRAINING: Without in any way limiting the Author's and Publisher's exclusive rights under copyright, any use of this publication to "train" generative artificial intelligence (AI) technologies to generate text is expressly prohibited. The Author and Publisher reserve all rights to license uses of this work for generative AI training and development of machine learning language models.

Typeset in Times New Roman 12/16 by
SJmagic DESIGN SERVICES, India.
Printed and bound in the UK by CPI Group (UK) Ltd.

The Publisher's authorised representative in the EU for product safety is Authorised Rep Compliance Ltd., Ground Floor, 71 Lower Baggot Street, Dublin D02 P593, Ireland.
www.arccompliance.com

For a complete list of Pen & Sword titles please contact
PEN & SWORD BOOKS LIMITED
George House, Units 12 & 13, Beevor Street, Off Pontefract Road, Barnsley, South Yorkshire, S71 1HN, England
E-mail: enquiries@pen-and-sword.co.uk
Website: www.pen-and-sword.co.uk

or

PEN AND SWORD BOOKS
1950 Lawrence Rd, Havertown, PA 19083, USA
E-mail: uspen-and-sword@casematepublishers.com
Website: www.penandswordbooks.com

Contents

I dedicate this book to both my wife Kelly, who gave me purpose and stood by me, and my fallen brothers in arms . . .

Gray Branfield	Joe Wessels
Neil Cameron	Ian Cameron
Seb Church	Jerry Roussow
Yves Mourang	Richie Coel
Sean Laver	Dave Shiels
Akihiko Saito	Nigel Clark
Morne Peters	Michael Fitzpatrick
Frederik Nel	Nic Coetzee
Geoff Fleck	Jo Bresler
Frankie Ricardo	Nick Crouch
Bevan Campbell	Martyn Butler
Jim Guthrie	Nick Ward
Norman Steinberg	Pete Curley

Disclaimer

This book is a work of nonfiction based on the personal experiences and recollections of the author. Names, identifying characteristics, locations, specific events, and certain operational details have been deliberately changed, omitted, or fictionalised to protect the identities, privacy, and confidentiality of individuals involved. Dialogue and incidents have been recreated from memory and, in some cases, condensed for narrative clarity.

The views, opinions, and perceptions expressed herein are solely those of the author and do not necessarily represent the official stance, policies, or perspectives of any employers, past or present, including military, security firms, or governmental agencies mentioned or implied within. Any resemblance to actual individuals, organisations, or events beyond those publicly known or recorded is purely coincidental and unintentional.

The author has taken careful measures to ensure that sensitive or confidential operational information is not disclosed. This publication is intended solely for the purpose of sharing the author's personal journey, insights, and reflections. It is not intended as a definitive historical account or an official representation of any operations, tactics, or procedures.

Readers are advised to consider the subjective nature of personal memoirs and exercise discretion accordingly.

Chapter 1

The Call

Tuesday afternoon, November 2003, Edinburgh, I'm having lunch with a friend when my phone rang. *It's a London number, I don't recognise it*, anyway, I'm tucking into a juicy burger, *I'm not answering*. It stopped, then immediately rang again. *Ok, someone really wants to talk to me . . .* 'Hello, is this Scott White?' a woman asked. 'Yes,' I replied. 'How can I help you?'

Her next question took me by surprise: 'Can you come down to London on Thursday?' I had no idea what this was about. Before I could ask, she hit me with something bigger. 'Oh, and are you available to deploy to Iraq on Saturday?'

I sat there, stunned. *Iraq? This Saturday?* I thought, 'That's not much notice,' I mumbled internally, my mind racing. But something about it felt compelling, too good to pass up. 'Yes, okay,' I said, still in shock, as though the gravity of what she was asking hadn't fully sunk in yet.

After what felt like the quickest Q&A I've ever had, I finished up lunch and headed home to book flights. *Was that it? Was that the interview? Is this a job offer, or just more talk? I didn't know.* In my line of work, nothing's real until there's a contract in your hand and your boots are on the ground. I've had plenty of promises before, nods, handshakes, 'you're our guy', only for it to vanish the next day. So, I didn't get carried away. No point. Until it's signed.

Thursday, I flew down on the red eye at 0600hrs, jumped on the train into the city and found the address, where I found myself sitting in a sleek, modern office block in the heart of London. The place felt worlds away from the reality I was about to step into. The bloke across from me introduced himself to me only as Nick. He shook my hand and said, 'Take a seat'. It was obvious he was an ex-army officer with the kind of calm, public schoolboy demeanour you'd expect, from someone who's been around the upper class most of his life. He's sat behind a small desk sipping on some sparkling water out of a glass in a bare office with blank walls, chatting in a way that suggested this wasn't just any old interview. It was surreal – here I was, in a space that reeked of privilege and comfort, and in 48 hours, I'd be heading straight into a war zone.

The conversation was short, almost unnervingly so. He asked a few pointed questions, assessing my background, experience, and readiness. 'You know what you're getting into?' he asked, leaning back in his chair, his gaze sharp. I nodded. I'd done my homework, had the training, knew the risks, and understood that this was no ordinary job.

He explained the job in a no-nonsense way, bullet-pointing the objectives, the risks, the chaos waiting on the ground. It was all very matter of fact, like we were discussing logistics for a business trip rather than stepping into one of the most dangerous places on Earth. 'Two days to get everything sorted,' he said, 'gear, travel, paperwork. You'll be briefed on the rest when you get there.'

I remember sitting there, absorbing the reality of it. There was no room for second thoughts now. The enormity of it all began to sink in. I wasn't just preparing for a trip, I was preparing to enter a war zone. I'd need to be ready for anything: the violence, the unpredictability, the sheer survival instinct I would need to rely on once the ground beneath me became hostile.

With that, the meeting was over. It felt strangely anticlimactic. I stood up, shook his hand, and walked out of that high-rise office, back into the bustling streets of London where people hurried along, oblivious to the storm I was about to walk into. Two days, that's all

I had to get my life in order, say my goodbyes, write my will, call my dentist to get my dental records, in case my teeth were the only way of identifying me, and prepare for whatever awaited me on the other side. And in that moment, I realised there was no turning back . . .

How the hell did Nick from London get my number? I didn't know him, and I'd never even heard of the guy. Turns out, it all traced back to a CP (Close Protection) job I did for MTV Europe. I was working alongside a cracking bloke called Jocky – ex-Royal Scots Captain, sharp as a blade, no bullshit, just a nice guy. We clicked straight away, same mindset, same sense of humour. One of the good ones.

Once the job wrapped, we went for a pint and started chatting about Iraq. Things were just starting to heat up over there for private military contractors, and he asked if it was something I'd ever think about doing.

Yeah, I considered it, but I asked him what he thought the money would be?

He reckoned companies were paying around seven to eight thousand a month. I nearly spat out my beer. 'Fuckin' hell, that's decent!' 'Aye, I'd consider it for that sort of money.'

Truth be told though, I'd already reached out to a firm called Sandline, a well-known PMC (Private Military Company) and had started putting the feelers out. It's not just the money to be honest, the whole adventure was appealing too.

At the time, I didn't think much of it. Just a casual chat over a drink. Jocky kept his cards close to his chest at this point.

What I didn't realise was that he had connections, one of his old Sandhurst mates was heading up recruitment for another Private Military Company and looking for men who could deploy at short notice.

A few weeks later, after he had a word with his contact, I got the call from Nick, and just like that, it was game on.

Saturday 0600hrs

My wife Sarah and I are already awake, but the house is quiet, wrapped in a strange mix of excitement and anxiety. Kyle, our four-year-old, plods through into our room, hair all messy and his eyes half shut. He smiles while climbing into bed with us as he usually does, snuggling in between us like it's any other day. We lie there together, Sarah and I just looking at one another. No words. Just the weight of the moment hanging in the air, a raw, unspoken emotion passing between us.

Kyle knows I'm leaving, though he doesn't quite understand why. At his age, he knows something is different, but the reality of it is still beyond him. As we lay there, my thoughts were racing. *Am I doing the right thing? Will I make it back? Will I see them again?* But there was no turning back now. The flights were booked, my bags were packed, and the decision had been made.

That afternoon, they came with me to the airport. In hindsight, it was the worst thing I could have done. I thought I could handle it; boy was I wrong. Saying goodbye was unbearable. While heading to the airport, we were laughing and joking in the car and keeping Kyle occupied singing songs. This soon changed when we got inside. Kyle clung to my leg, his little arms wrapped tightly around me, and Sarah, holding back tears, tried to stay strong for his sake. It felt like my heart was being ripped out my chest, leaving them there. But I had to go.

The first farewell is always a blur, a strange mix of emotions and actions that you're barely present for. Sarah and Kyle walked me all the way up to security. We shared one last kiss, trying to keep it together. Sarah was already starting to break, tears silently running down her face, and as soon as Kyle saw them, he couldn't hold it in either.

I gave one final wave and turned to walk through the gate. But I hadn't even made it halfway when I heard him – Kyle, screaming, his little voice cutting through the noise of the airport. 'Daddy! Don't go, please! Daddy!' His cries were desperate, heart-wrenching.

I froze. I could feel my own heart breaking. I turned back, and before I knew it, he was running straight through security. Nothing mattered in that moment except him. I dropped my bag and scooped him up, clutching him tightly as tears streamed down my face. I kissed him, holding him so close that it was hard to tell where his tears ended and mine began. The world around us felt distant, surreal. Everything seemed to slow down.

Sarah, usually the one to fall apart, became the strong one right then. She had to. She coaxed Kyle with a packet of chewing gum, trying to calm him down. 'It's only for a few months,' I whispered to him, though it felt like a lie, even to me. I tried to smile, make light of it all, but it felt hollow. Sarah played along, pretending everything was fine. She tried to hide the storm of emotions behind her eyes, but I saw it. We both knew this wasn't just some quick trip, but we kept up the facade for Kyle's sake.

Eventually, I had to go. There was no more stalling. Sarah gave me one final look; her eyes filled with love and fear. Kyle's grip loosened as he focused on his gum, but I could still feel his small hand in mine, unwilling to let go until the very last second. It was the hardest thing I'd ever done, walking away from them, from everything that mattered most.

As I approached the departure gate, I immediately noticed a few other guys standing around, shifting their weight from foot to foot, their eyes scanning the crowd. We all had similar bergens and packs – rugged, heavy duty. More telling, though, was the look on their faces. Steely eyes, unsure, probably feeling the same way I was, and in that moment, I knew, these were my people. We were all in the same boat – or, rather, the same plane – headed into the unknown.

Alright, I thought, *who here can I talk to?* Maybe a conversation could help ease the tension, calm the nerves a little, or at the very least make this whole thing feel a bit more manageable. I scanned the faces, trying to size them up. Most looked like former soldiers, maybe contractors. Others were harder to read. But the anxious energy was unmistakable, and it made me feel a bit less alone.

Before I could figure out who to approach, the boarding call came, and suddenly we were shuffling down the jet bridge, no turning back now. Next thing I knew, I was strapped into a seat heading on a Royal Jordanian flight, lifting off from Heathrow and heading toward Amman. The hum of the engines was the only constant in the swirl of thoughts racing through my mind. It was happening. This is it!

How scared was I? *Fucking shitting myself,* if I'm being honest. My stomach was in knots, and my palms were sweaty. I couldn't shake the feeling that everything was about to change. Every worst, case scenario was running through my head on a loop, what if I didn't make it back? What if something went horribly wrong?

I looked around the plane. Some of the other guys were fidgeting, some pretending to be cool, flipping through in-flight magazines like they weren't about to step into a war zone. But I could see it in their eyes too, the uncertainty. None of us knew what awaited us on the ground, and that unspoken dread hung heavy in the cabin.

The flight attendants walked by with carts of drinks, but I couldn't even think about eating or drinking. My mind was a storm of thoughts, my family, the risk, the job, the unknown. I tried to calm myself down, tried to remind myself that this is what I trained for, that I was prepared. But still, the fear was real, and it wasn't going away anytime soon.

I leaned back in my seat and stared out the window as the plane cut through the clouds. In a matter of hours, we'd be on the ground in the Middle East, and from there, the real journey would begin. Whatever happened next, I knew one thing for sure: this was no ordinary adventure.

Chapter 2

Touchdown

Sunday 9 November 2003 – 0400hrs

It's still dark when we are met at Amman airport in Jordan, by one bloke in a black cot vest, board in hand with loads of names. He speedily escorts us out of the airport, checks our names on the list before introducing us to Gaz and Paul. They are the blokes that have been here for a bit and will escort us in local vehicles to our first meeting point. I notice that some of the names on the list are not here, probably decided to bug out, I mean who in their right minds would dive into the unknown not knowing if they would return?

Words can't quite capture the feeling as we roll into Baghdad. It's overwhelming, horrific and electrifying all at once. The fear of the unknown hangs heavy over me, settling in my gut like a stone. But there's something else too, something that has my hands trembling slightly. It's excitement, the kind of excitement that comes from knowing I'm exactly where I've wanted to be for years. I can't help but feel that strange mix of terror and anticipation building inside me. I'm finally here, in the thick of it.

There are four of us travelling together. Neil, Gareth, Tony, and I are in a local 4x4, and I have been on the go now for 26 hours straight. The exhaustion is seeping into every bone, every muscle is heavy and slow, but the adrenaline kick now and again keeps us awake. We're packed into this local car, part of a ten-vehicle convoy, each one filled with new blood like us. No one says much. We're too wired for that, or maybe too tired. I keep drifting off, my head bobbing against the window, eyes slipping closed as I think of home, of what it was like before all this. But every time I wake up, the reality slams into me like a punch to the gut. This is real. We're here. This isn't some dream I'll wake from.

As the sun rises, we see the reality of war. Baghdad is spread out before us, and it's nothing like I expected. The destruction is everywhere. It's inescapable. Brick houses line the streets, but they're barely standing, riddled with bullet holes, some looking like they've been through the grinder. Others aren't even houses anymore, just wrecks, charred and smoking, gutted by fire or bombs, leaving nothing but skeletal remains. The place smells like ash and burnt metal, the air in humid and the smell is something you can't explain. It's hard to believe people lived here, that this was once a functioning city. Now, it feels like a graveyard. A place emptied of life but full of danger.

I can feel that vulnerability gnawing at me. We don't have any weapons yet, and it's like walking through a battlefield naked. Every time I look out the window, I wonder what's lurking around the next corner, in the shadows of those ruined buildings. Both Gaz and Paul, our own CP guys, seem calm, though. They don't look worried at all. These guys are hard as nails, kitted out with all the gear and weapons we're still waiting to get. They look like they've seen it all before. Their faces are unreadable, but they've got that mercenary look down to a T, even the signature SAS tash. It gives me some comfort, knowing they're with us, but it doesn't make the feeling of being exposed any less real.

I keep telling myself that this is what I trained for, that I made this choice. But it doesn't stop my nerves from fraying a little more with every mile we cover. I just want to get to the base. I want to be somewhere solid, somewhere I can grab a weapon and feel like I've got a fighting chance if something goes wrong. Every minute in this convoy feels like an eternity but all I can do is sit here, watching the city unfold in front of me, reminding myself that this is what I wanted. This is what I'm here for.

1600hrs

We have a local Iraqi driving us down from Amman, he looks like he's about to pass out from exhaustion. He's been behind the wheel for 12 hours straight, most of it through the night. The rest of us have been drifting in and out of sleep, but I've just woken up, and something's not right. My eyes snap open, and the first thing I see is him, his head nodding forward, eyes barely open, and we're barrelling down the road at 80mph we're heading straight for the back of a truck up ahead. I shout out to Neil, who was nodding off too, in the front seat, and he reacts instantly, grabbing the wheel and shouting to the driver just in time. we swerve, and for a second, everything feels like it's hanging in the balance. My heart is pounding in my chest, and I can hear Tony and Gareth cursing under their breath.

We can't stop, though. It's too dangerous out here to pull over, not with where we are and everything that's going on. So, we do the only thing we can, we splash the driver's face with water, trying to shake him out of his stupor. It's a temporary fix, but we don't have any other options. All I can think is that it'd be Sod's Law to come all this way to Iraq and get killed in a fucking car accident before we've even started the job.

We push on, all of us on edge now, eyes wide open, hoping like hell we make it the rest of the way in one piece.

Monday 24 November 2003

We rolled into Baghdad late last night, finally pulling up at this dingy motel called Al Dulami. It's the kind of place that feels like it's seen too much, worn down and grimy, with a smell of decay. Apparently, it's owned by one of Saddam Hussein's cousins, which doesn't do much to make it any more welcoming. But after the hell of the journey, it's a bed, and right now, that will do for me.

I've managed to gel with a couple of the lads here, Neil, another Scottish bloke from Edinburgh, and Bob, ex-Black Watch then Special Air Service, from Dundee. Neil is a tall guy with a hard face and quite an arrogant demeanour and Bob is a short fit wee guy, someone you wouldn't expect to be in the SAS that's for sure. Bob and I instantly clicked, I just knew we would be good mates. We share a room, not that there's much to it, but it's a bit of space to crash. We managed to scrounge up some food before hitting the sack. I was so knackered that I didn't even care about the state of the place.

That is until I wake up to the sound of gunfire right outside the window. It's unnerving, to say the least, but part of me is calm. This is what we signed up for, better get used to it.

I'm sitting in the motel, waiting for breakfast before we move out to Basra. The plan is for half of us to stay in Baghdad, while the other half, including me, head south. When breakfast comes, it's a joke – some stale bread, one boiled egg, and a wedge of cheese that looks like it's been sitting around for days. They give us a cup of tea too, though it's so weak it hardly deserves the name. Still, it's something to put in the stomach before we head out into whatever waits for us next.

Tuesday 25 November 2003, 0600hrs – Basra

We've made it to Basra, and at first glance, it's a bit of a different vibe than Baghdad. There's a calmness here, a sense of order, and I can't help but think it's because the Brits are holding things down. It feels safer, at least at first glance. We're staying at this place called the Mirbad Hotel, right in the centre of town. The whole thing is fortified like a bunker, with a massive brick wall and barbed wire fencing around it. Armed Iraqi guards, ones we pay to watch the place, stand on patrol 24/7, which gives it the illusion of security. But I've been here just long enough to know that safety is just a feeling that can disappear in a heartbeat.

As soon as we settle in, we're handed our weapons, if you can call them that. They gave us these ancient AK-47s, the kind you'd expect to see in a museum, with only three mags and 90 rounds each. Then there are the pistols, old Russian Makarovs and I swear, they look like they were dug up from the Iran-Iraq War. Rusted, worn, and barely functional. But it's better than nothing, Bob and I got to work, stripping them down and giving them a good clean ready for use.

The hotel next door didn't fare so well. It was blown to shit by a car bomb just four days ago, and you can still see the rubble, scorched earth, and debris scattered everywhere. And, of course, it's still Eid, their version of Christmas, so everything's shut down tight. Despite the holiday, we've got a task tomorrow. There's no downtime in this place, not when everything feels like it could erupt at any second.

Last night, as I lay down to sleep, that feeling of safety evaporated. The sounds of gunfire echoed all around us, constant and unnerving. So much for thinking Basra was safer. That illusion was shattered quickly. I'm lying there, listening to the barrage of gunfire ringing out in the distance, and all I can think is that this place is as dangerous as anywhere else. Maybe the Brits being here gives off the vibe of control, but in reality, it's the same chaos, just dressed differently.

Wednesday 26 November 2003, 0500hrs

This morning, we all mustered in the car park of the hotel for our first mission. Everything here feels like it's held together with string and tape. It's a well-known company, but I think this set-up was done in a rush, our weapons are barely functional, we haven't had a chance to test them, we've got no body armour, and we're relying on a bunch of locals with their own soft-skinned vehicles to escort our clients. It's bare bones, but it's what we've got to work with. There's no sense complaining; at the end of the day, we're getting paid well for this, and the adrenaline rush is enough to make up for it.

My job here is Close Protection for the US Army Corps of Engineers and their contractors. It's all about keeping them alive while they try to rebuild parts of this broken country. They're here to inspect and rebuild the main power line running from Baghdad to Basra. Our convoy is made up of two vehicles: the first has the Team leader with our principal, and me in the chase car bringing up the rear, four or five in each vehicle all armed, It's not exactly a military-grade operation, but it's functional, barely.

Today's mission was simple on paper: head to Basra Airport, we have a building there which serves as our HQ, pick up an American engineer, and escort him down to the Kuwait military border. But out here, nothing's simple. The road to Kuwait is littered with potential ambush points. Every turn, every bend in the road, could be the start of an attack. We even spotted a couple of stingers, crude roadblocks, set up on the way, though luckily, we avoided anything more serious. Basra doesn't have the full-scale terror networks like the north has, well, not yet anyway, but the local militia are brutal enough. They rob, kill, and pillage for money. To them, we're just targets of opportunity.

On the way back to the hotel the main road was closed off, a fresh IED (Improvised Explosive Device) had just detonated. We didn't get any word on casualties yet.

I'm partnered up with big Gerry Russouw, an incredible bloke from Rhodesia. He's about 52, year, old, stands at 6ft 3. Powerful frame with a full grey goatee beard and the kind of presence that commands respect. Big man with an even bigger heart. Gerry was a Special Forces sergeant with the Selous Scouts for 17 years. He's been through three wars, and you can feel the experience radiating off him. He's calm under pressure, always aware of what's going on, I learn so much from him, he's almost like a father figure. You would see Gerry with a smoke hanging from his mouth kicking the tyres before every mission.

The rest of the blokes are a diverse mix, former SAS, Paras, Guards, Foreign Legion, and Royal Marines. A broad range of backgrounds, forming what feels like an international unit of seasoned veterans. It's the real-life version of *The Expendables* – minus the designer gear and tattoo clichés. Everyone brings their own specialist skill set to the table.

For now, I'm keeping a low profile, playing the grey man, staying observant. I'll take my time to assess the teams, figure out the dynamics, and learn who's who. Out here, survival depends on understanding the environment and knowing who you can trust. So, I'll let them do what they do, and I'll focus on my own role. Time will reveal how it all plays out.

I'm attached to Alpha Team, a good bunch of guys. We've got Bret, ex Green Jacket, a short, heavyset guy with a broken nose and a bit of a bald spot. He's from London originally but lives in Thailand now with his wife. Bret's got a wicked sense of humour, always a sexual inuendo, and the lads have nicknamed him the 'GIMP'. The kind of guy that should be locked in a cupboard and fed once or twice a day. A real deviant, but in the best possible way. He keeps morale up with his dark twisted jokes.

Sam and I have grown close. He's from London as well, also ex Green Jacket. Sam's one of those genuinely good blokes, always thinking about others and making sure everyone's all right. He's got this natural charisma, cracking jokes, and keeping the mood light when we need it most. But there's no mistaking that when the shit hits the fan, Sam's the kind of guy you want next to you. There's a quiet steeliness about him, you just know he'll step up when things go sideways.

As for Basra, it's the arsehole of the earth, no other way to put it. The stench is unbearable, raw sewage flows right alongside the roads, and as the temperature climbs, the smell thickens, making it hard to breathe. It clings to everything, this rotten, pungent scent that's impossible to escape. If you can imagine a scrap yard dumped in the middle of the desert, you'd be close. Wrecked cars, old military tanks, and rusted heaps of steel are strewn everywhere. It's like the remnants of war have been left to rot in the sun. Nothing much is left standing, the clay-built houses are mostly blown to hell, just rubble now.

The streets are filled with kids, some as young as five or six, wearing old clothing that was obviously handed down from older brothers as it hangs on their small frames. They are all begging for water. It's heartbreaking. Just yesterday, I saw a woman by the roadside, holding a baby in her arms, pleading for help. It's moments like that when the weight of this place hits you. You feel ashamed, helpless even. There's nothing we can do, and it's annoying. The worst part is knowing that even when these kids get their hands on some water or food, the older men, maybe their fathers, uncles, who knows, beat it out of them. You watch as these grown men kick the hell out of them, snatching away whatever scraps they've managed to beg for. It's brutal, but it's just the way things are here. Survival in this place is a cold, hard reality, and no one is spared, not even the kids.

Every day in Basra feels like a fight, whether it's with the heat, the stench, or just the sight of so much desperation.

Every morning at 0500hrs. like clockwork, the wailing starts. It pours out of loudspeakers all over the city, the call to prayer, echoing through the streets. The local muezzin's voice, a way of waking people up, I guess. To these people, it's just part of life, but for us, it's a harsh reminder of how different this world is. Religion is everything to them, woven into the fabric of their existence. But it's hard to grasp sometimes, watching them cling to faith when all the praying in the world doesn't seem to help their situation. The devastation, the poverty, the death and destruction, it's everywhere. It makes you wonder how they can keep believing when their world is in pieces around them.

Just yesterday, we had this 10-year-old boy hanging around near the military border between Iraq and Kuwait. A scrawny kid, clothes hanging off him, eyes full of something too old for his years. He comes up to us, bold as brass, and says he knows where Saddam is hiding. 'FUCK SADDAM,' he spits, with more venom than I've ever seen from a kid that age. He tells us that for $1,000, he'll tell us where to find him. The hatred for Saddam around here is palpable. They despise him, he's the reason their lives are in ruins, and even the kids feel it. You can see it in their eyes, the way they talk about him. It's raw, unfiltered hatred.

Today's mission is a different one. We're heading to the Safwan military crossing, the main entry point into Iraq from Kuwait. We've to pick up an American engineer from the Army Corps of Engineers. These guys, I swear, they get on our nerves, always showing up in full military kit, helmets, flak jackets, the works, like they're heading into battle. But it puts us at risk. Out here, subtlety is survival, and these guys stick out like sore thumbs.

We keep telling them, 'Take the helmet off, throw a shirt over your uniform, blend in.' But they refuse every time. 'We're proud of our uniform,' they say. Proud? More like arrogant. It's not about pride out here; it's about staying alive. They honestly think they're invincible, marching around in full gear like a target. They don't realise, or maybe they don't care, that when they make themselves stand out; they're making us all sitting ducks. Every time we roll out with them, it feels like we're just waiting to be smacked.

Saturday 29 November 2003

Our first task today was to escort a civilian Perini engineer named Tom Russell up to inspect a power line. Seemed simple enough, but things rarely go as planned out here. We arrived at base camp from the hotel and were stood down almost immediately, told to hold tight. Intelligence had come in, there was an ambush waiting for us up ahead. EOD (Explosive Ordinance Disposal – 'the bomb squad') had found a crude bomb dug into the road, just lying in wait for us to drive right into it.

With that mission scrapped, we were reassigned to escort a six-truck convoy back to the Kuwait border. No issues with that, it's only a 40-minute run, and the road's relatively secure, at least by local standards. The convoy moved smoothly, no problems along the way. But as we got closer to the border, things started to pick up. The middle reservation of the road was packed with kids, dozens of them, all smiling and waving at us, holding out their hands like they're expecting something. They all shout 'Maya', 'Maya' which translates to water in English.

Once we returned to base, we got hit with another task: another convoy of trucks needed escorting to the border. We loaded up, ready to go, but as we were leaving HQ, everything ground to a halt. The checkpoint at the gate was backed up, some bastard had left a car bomb right there. We were stuck, waiting for the EOD team to come in and deal with it. They blew it up, but by the time the area was cleared, it was too late to complete the mission.

After we were done for the day and heading back to the hotel, things got heated. Bret, who was in a car two vehicles ahead of us, had some Iraqi pull a pistol on him in the middle of city traffic, classic bit of road rage, but out here, it's not just about shouting and swearing. The guy was waving his pistol around like he was ready to use it. We gave them some backup from our car, we pulled up beside him, leaning out the windows with our AKs ready. Once the gunman saw that, he backed off quick. Changed his mind, thankfully.

Sunday 30 November 2003 0600hrs

We left the hotel early, heading straight to HQ. First thing we did was sneak into the American base next door for a quick breakfast. It's a bit of a perk. We get to eat their food, which is leagues better than anything we get outside the base. After breakfast, we headed to the TV room, where we caught some Sky News. More of the same: two ambushes reported. One in Tikrit, Saddam's hometown, and another in Baghdad. No surprises there, ambushes are a daily, sometimes hourly occurrence around here. It's the way of life in Iraq.

Our task today was to look after Tom Russell again. He's a good guy, works for Perini, a huge American reconstruction company. He's taken a liking to us and has asked if we could be his permanent security detail. It's a compliment, really. He trusts us, and out here, trust is worth more than gold. Today's mission was a bit different. We were heading to a small village called Garamesh, a shantytown on the outskirts of Basra, and easily the most dangerous spot in the city right now. The place is lawless, crawling with gangs and desperate people.

We had a meeting scheduled with a sheikh, a big deal around here. As soon as we pulled up, we were swarmed. Kids came running first, dozens of them, curious and excited. Then the adults followed, gathering around, watching us closely. It felt tense for a second, so we went into formation, AKs ready, keeping Tom in the middle. It's instinct at this point, never trust a crowd, especially in a place like this.

But as we stood there, we started to realise there was no real danger. These people weren't hostile, just curious. They've probably never seen guys like us up close before. The kids were wide-eyed, some laughing, some just staring. The adults, on the other hand, were nervous. You could see it in their eyes, they live a different life, one stuck in the past. It felt like we'd stepped into another world, a place untouched by time. Ancient ways of life clashing with the chaos of modern war. The whole situation was surreal, but thankfully, it went off without a hitch. For now, anyway.

On the way back, we came across something that'll haunt me for a long time, a bus crash, and not just any crash. The bus had come off a bridge, flipped onto its roof. It was like a scene out of a horror movie. There were bodies everywhere, kids, mostly. Lifeless, scattered across the road, some still tangled in the wreckage. Blood was smeared all over the twisted metal and the pavement, pooling under the wreck. It was a massacre, pure and simple.

I can't even describe the feeling. It hit me hard, a pit forming in my stomach. These weren't soldiers or combatants, just kids. Innocent lives, snuffed out in an instant. It was chaos. The sight of their small bodies, lifeless and broken, burned into my mind.

The worst part? We couldn't stop. We wanted to; God knows we did. Every instinct screamed to pull over, to try and do something, anything. But it was too dangerous. This stretch of road was notorious for ambushes, and stopping could have made us sitting ducks as local militia hide hoping we stop then ambush you. So, we had to keep going, drive past the horror and push down the guilt that came with it. That was one of the hardest things I've had to do so far.

Monday 1 December 2003 0600hrs

Gerry pulled some strings and managed to lock us in as Tom Russell's permanent detail. He refuses to go out without us now, which speaks volumes about how much he trusts the team. Today's mission was a bit different. We were tasked with escorting four mobile homes from the Kuwait border to Garamesh, the same village we were in yesterday. The Americans are setting up a small base there, trying to get some kind of foothold in the area.

As we rolled into Garamesh, the familiar sight greeted us, the local tribe mobbed us almost instantly. They see us as something between a curiosity and a lifeline. I spotted a boy who looked about Kyle's age barefoot, with only a tattered T-shirt hanging off his thin frame. He had nothing. Total poverty doesn't even begin to describe what these people are living in. It's beyond comprehension.

I knelt down, trying to speak to him, maybe offer him a bit of kindness. I pulled out a sweet from my pocket, hoping to make him smile. But instead, he burst into tears, sobbing uncontrollably. His father, if you could even call him that, thought it was hilarious. He grabbed the boy by the arms and held him up like an animal, laughing while the kid screamed. The sight of it turned my stomach. I clenched my fists, every part of me wanting to knock the bastard out right there and then. But what can you do? This is their reality, and it's brutal.

It's easy to keep it together during the day, when everything's happening around you. But at night, when you're lying in bed, alone with your thoughts, that's when it hits you. The weight of it all. The helplessness. These kids have nothing, no future, no hope. It's soul-crushing. One man I spoke to told me how Saddam had murdered his wife and baby daughter. It was sickening, hearing the raw pain in his voice. And that's when it hit me, I realised, deep down, that we were right to invade. These people have suffered beyond belief under Saddam's dictatorship. He would cut off their food, water, and electricity, punishing the south for being Shia Muslims. He starved and tortured them, kept them living in fear.

Tuesday 2 December 2003

We headed back to the local shanty town again, as Tom was getting deeper into setting up his camp there. By now, the routine had become familiar. The kids were waiting for us, but they were more relaxed this time, no longer as nervous or curious. They seemed to have warmed up to us. They'd smile and wave, and all they wanted were pictures with us, like we were celebrities or something. It was strange, seeing their faces light up at something as simple as a photo when their lives were so bleak.

We started bringing water, food, and sweets for them, little things that made them so happy. It was the least we could do, but even these small gestures seemed to mean the world to them. You could see it in their eyes; gratitude mixed with curiosity. It's hard to grasp how much they've suffered, but these little moments made you feel like, for once, you were doing something good in a place so full of misery.

Later, we met up with another one of our teams from Al Qurna, a city north of Basra, and had lunch at one of Saddam's old palaces. The sheer size of the place was mind-blowing – huge, opulent, a reminder of the obscene wealth and power Saddam once wielded while his people starved. Gerry, with his endless knowledge of the region, pointed out something that took me by surprise. Just outside the palace, where the Tigris River runs to our right, was the proposed site of the biblical Garden of Eden. It felt surreal, we're not far from a place with such historical and religious significance yet surrounded by war and devastation. Al Qurna is where the Euphrates and Tigris rivers meet, and this is supposedly where civilization began?

Everyone knows about the Garden of Eden, it used to be a pilgrimage for Christians many years ago, but Saddam had it desecrated when he came to power. The idea of seeing it in person was too tempting to pass up, even with the danger that came with it. Gerry and I asked one of our local translators if they could take us there, and to our surprise, they said they knew the way. The whole concept of being in such a historically significant place was mind, blowing, so we decided to risk it.

When we finally pulled up to the site, it wasn't quite what I'd imagined. There was a brick wall surrounding a quad-like area, and it didn't look like much at first glance. 'Is this it?' I asked, a little disappointed. I expected something grander, more fitting for the mythical Garden of Eden. But sometimes, history doesn't look the way you picture it.

We walked into the quad, and in the middle of the space stood a tree. An old, gnarled, dead tree, twisted and bare. Gerry looked at me and asked if I knew what it was. When I shook my head, he told me it was the Adam Tree – the very tree that, according to local tradition, was tied to the Garden of Eden in the Bible. I couldn't believe it. Standing there, looking at that ancient tree, I felt a strange sense of awe. It wasn't about whether or not the stories were true, it was the weight of history, of belief, of everything this place represented.

I wanted something to take with me, a piece of this place, this moment. Something real. One of the local kids had wandered over, curious about what these Westerners were up to. I handed him my knife and nodded to the tree. 'Go on, mate. Grab me a bit.' He climbed up without question, sliced off a few dry branches, and passed them down. Just a handful of dead wood, but it meant something. Proof I'd stood there. That I'd seen it with my own eyes. He handed them to me, and I pocketed the wood then gathered a few stones from the base of the tree as mementos. Later, I had a local craftsman carve me a small Arabic box, and now I keep those pieces of the Adam Tree and stones inside it. It's strange to think I hold something from a place so deeply intertwined with the story of humanity. Standing there, in the supposed Garden of Eden, made me feel connected to something far greater than the war and chaos around us. It's a memory I'll never forget.

Thursday 4 December 2003 0600hrs

Today's detail with Tom Russell had us heading back to Garamesh, the usual routine. We made a stop at Al Amarah, escorting another electrician from Perini along the way with some trucks full of equipment. Everything seemed routine, no issues on the road, no ambushes, no close calls. When we pulled into Al Amarah, we encountered two trucks from India, clearly out of their depth and terrified. The drivers were practically begging us to escort them to the border. You could see the panic etched on their faces. The thought of travelling at night without any protection in this part of the world, it was enough to put the fear of death into anyone. I could feel their desperation, and for a second, I thought about it, but they weren't part of our detail, and it wasn't our call to make.

We left them there, sending them off on their own, knowing full well what could happen. A bit shit, but we had a job to do, and it wasn't them. A few hours later, we woke up to the news that those two trucks were ambushed overnight. The drivers were killed, and the trucks were stolen. Just like that. Do I feel guilty? Of course, but what can I do?

The real test came on the way back. We found ourselves driving through the dark, something you never want to do out here. Travelling at night is practically a death sentence if you're not properly equipped, and with seven trucks in tow, we were struggling to maintain control. The tension was thick, and every shadow on the road felt like an ambush waiting to happen. We had no choice but to call HQ for backup. There was just too much ground to cover, and in the dark, it was impossible to keep an eye on everything.

Luckily, we had picked up some grenades earlier in the day from the local market, so at least we were a bit more kitted out than usual. Having those in hand made us feel a little more secure, but the relief didn't come until we made it back to camp. Even Adnan, my local driver, let out a heavy sigh when we rolled through the gates, and Talib, one of our local guards, who we now call 'Rambo' because of his obsession with American action movies, looked like he could finally breathe again. He talks a big game, loves to act like the tough guy, but when it comes down to it, everyone's feeling the pressure out here.

That night, sitting back at camp, I couldn't help but think about those Indian truck drivers again. It's a brutal world here, and sometimes, no matter what you do, people don't make it.

Chapter 3

The Baghdad Run

Sunday 7 December 2003

No one with half a brain was volunteering to run the gauntlet from Basra to Baghdad. It was the most dangerous stretch of road in Iraq at this time, six hours of pure adrenaline and risk. And with soft skin vehicles, if you were attacked, you had no chance of survival. But when the PM (Project Manager) asked for volunteers, Gerry and I didn't hesitate. Call it madness, call it whatever you want, we signed up, no questions asked.

The mission was straightforward on paper: escort six trucks loaded with crucial electrical gear for the reconstruction efforts. Gerry took the lead in his Land Cruiser, with the trucks following, and I brought up the rear. Felt more like we were shepherding a flock of sheep than leading a convoy. That gear was valuable, so valuable that every lowlife insurgent in the region would want a piece of it.

We hadn't even left Basra before the first hiccup. Two of the trucks were running low on diesel. Are you kidding me? In a war zone, and these idiots hadn't topped up their tanks. It meant a pit stop in town, a risk we couldn't afford, but had no choice. Then, to top it off, one of the Iraqi drivers suddenly veered off from the convoy without a word. Turns out he decided to make a quick detour to visit his wife!

Gerry stayed with the other trucks while I went after the runaway. When I caught up with him, I was fucking raging. I yanked him out of the cab, gave him a few slaps, and made it clear: if he tried that again, I wouldn't hesitate to put a bullet in him myself. This wasn't a game, and he needed to know that. He said sorry and realised he was wrong.

We pushed on but had to call it for the night when we hit Al Amarah. We were losing light, so we decided to find a hotel, if you could call it that, a complete shithole down some dingy side street. One of our local guys went in to check if it was safe enough. 'Reasonably safe,' he said. Yeah, sure. But what choice did we have?

Hotels like this don't want anything to do with us. They're terrified of being caught helping coalition forces, it's a death sentence if the wrong people find out. I asked the owner for a bottle of water, and he brought me some brown sludge in a cup. No thanks. I wasn't about to gamble my life on that. The bed? Wet, stinking of rot. I didn't care. I slept in full kit, rifle in hand.

Monday 8 December 2003 0500hrs

We set off at first light, hoping the rest of the journey would be smoother. We finally hit Baghdad at 2100hrs after a gruelling 16-hour drive. It should have been quicker, but these bloody Iraqi drivers keep stopping for picnics like we're on some sort of scenic road trip, not rolling through a war zone. As we roll into the city, it looks completely wrecked, like something out of a movie. It's only been about a month since I got here, but I can already tell things have shifted. The tension in the air is thicker, and the city feels like it's on the verge of tearing itself apart.

Apache gunships are circling overhead like vultures, and gunfire echoes through the streets constantly. Baghdad isn't just dangerous; it's a war zone in every sense. Our base is a house in the Karrada district, smack in the middle of the RED ZONE, not far from GREEN ZONE where the Americans have their little fortified paradise. The house is right next to the Ministry of Electricity, which is basically a massive bullseye for anyone looking to lob a mortar or two.

Like us, there is a local guard force around the place, armed to the teeth with heavy weapons. It needs to be because this area gets hit regularly. We're surrounded by government officials' homes, and they seem to attract more than their fair share of trouble.

Gerry and I, in need of a break, head down to the local shop at the end of the road to grab some smokes. It's only 100 yards or so, should be no problem, right? wrong. As we're heading back, some twat decides to take pot shots at us, two rounds, sounded like a pistol. Just another day in Baghdad, nearly slotted for a pack of smokes. I couldn't help but laugh about it afterward – imagine that on my headstone . . . he literally did die from smoking.

Tuesday 9 December 2003

We set off from Baghdad at 1000hrs, heading down south to Basra again and I'm not even nervous about the locals; it's the Americans I'm worried about now. They'll shoot anyone who looks remotely suspicious, and that includes us. We're dressed like Iraqis, rolling in local cars, and armed with AKs, which makes us prime targets. We have Flash cards that we produce when confronted by Military. It's an orange A4 laminated sheet and a Union Flag. The Yanks don't take chances, and with tanks and gunships everywhere, it feels like we're walking on eggshells.

We're about two hours out from Basra, just as the sun starts dipping low in the sky, when Gerry radios in: 'HOSTILES AHEAD . . . Stand by . . '

I look ahead and see them, twelve masked blokes standing in the road, some in military gear, others in God knows what. There's three on either side of the road and six standing smack in the middle. My gut tightens, and I think to myself, *this is it*. Rambo and I cock our weapons, this is going to get messy.

But as we get closer, something strange happens, they lower their weapons and wave us through. I can hardly believe it. Turns out they're Iraqi Special Police or Army, although you'd never guess it from the way they're dressed. They have been tasked to try and stop local militias from attacking apparently. They have no proper uniforms; just whatever military gear they can get their hands on. They look more like militia than anything else.

Once we pass through, we stop at the Brit camp in Al Amarah to report what happened. Their CO says they've been given orders to shoot anyone who isn't easily recognisable. It's mad, anyone can pull on a uniform and set up an ambush.

We finally get back to HQ, only to be hit with more bad news. Al-Qaeda's been regrouping here in Basra, and their latest mission is to target 'soft targets' – basically, us. Westerners, especially those working on rebuilding the infrastructure, are now top of their hit list. The water plant next to our base is on the list, too, along with our hotel. And anyone in a 4x4 is a walking bullseye, which, again, is us.

The kidnap threat is through the roof now, and the whole team is on edge. No one's taking any chances anymore. It feels like we're all just waiting for something to kick off, and when it does, there's no doubt there'll be casualties.

Saturday 13 December 2003 0600hrs

I've got a bad case of gastric flu, been up all, night shitting and spewing, I feel like I'm being wrung out from the inside. I tried heading to Basra International Airport (HQ) in the morning, but I barely made it halfway down the stairs before turning back. I'm in no shape for anything right now. I managed to crawl into bed, hoping to sleep it off.

1100hrs, I'm jolted awake by the unmistakable sound of gunfire. Here we go again . . . but this is in the hotel complex?

Still in just my boxers, I stumble out of bed, dizzy and dripping with cold sweat. My legs feel like jelly, but I force myself to throw on my boots and grab my weapons. I'm in no state to fight, but instinct kicks in. I run up to the roof, trying not to pass out, to see what the hell is going on. There's chaos down in the streets, loads of Iraqis firing AKs into the air.

Leaning over the rooftop, I spot Sam down in the car park. I shout down to him, 'What the fuck is going on?' He looks up with the biggest grin and yells, 'They got the bastard, Saddam has been captured!'

I can't believe it. Saddam, the dictator we've all been after, is finally in custody. It's surreal being here in the middle of it all as it happens. I know the next few days are going to be mental, everyone's either celebrating or causing chaos. Gunfire's constant, people are out in the streets, shouting and firing in all directions. We decide it's probably smart to lie low for a couple of days and wait out.

In the aftermath, things get even weirder. We spend a few days talking to the locals, trying to get a sense of how they feel about Saddam's capture. Just a few days ago, most of them wanted the man dead. But now, there's a different mood, humiliation. They're ashamed of how he's been paraded on international TV by the Americans, made to look weak. It's like the propaganda backfired. Instead of feeling relieved, a lot of Iraqis are more pissed off at the Americans than ever. The Yanks have a real knack for stirring up resentment when they least need it.

Thursday 18 December 2003

Things have taken a turn for the worse. We've been told we need to evacuate the hotel, ASAP. Intel says Al-Qaeda's been snapping pictures of us coming and going, and it looks like they're planning an attack. Apparently, they've set up across the street, and we could be in the firing line any day now. Can't say I'm surprised, it's been tense, but this just kicked everything up a notch.

We've relocated to three rental houses in the centre of Basra. Not exactly luxury, but considering the alternatives, they're not bad. No beds, no water, and no electricity yet, but at least we've got somewhere relatively safe to lay low. There's 30 of us, so it's 10 blokes per house, two to a room. Luckily, Sam is here along with some South Africans, French and Bret. All the blokes are good lads but for now the only thing on my mind is the bog situation, I can't handle shitting in a hole in the floor. Lucky for us, our house has Western, style toilets. Absolute magic.

Gerry and I have shacked up in the same room. Both of us snore like a couple of wild boars, so at least we won't be keeping anyone else awake. For now, it's just about getting through the next few days in one piece. Things are escalating, and it feels like we're sitting on a powder keg.

Thursday 25 December 2003 (Christmas Day)

I have awoken today to the strangest of feelings. It's Christmas Day, I so much want to be home to see my family, I wish I could see my boy open his presents and feel the hugs from him as his wee face lights up. I will have to settle for a Skype video call, as we are a couple of hours ahead, I still have to wait an hour or so before I can see them.

If anyone had told me a year ago that I'd be spending Christmas here in Iraq, I'd have said, 'Bollocks!' But here we are, in the thick of it. The latest news we received from Baghdad, was that a frag grenade was lobbed over the wall last night, and then someone opened fire into our compound. Chaos erupted. Twelve of the lads scrambled up to the roof, taking defensive positions, and let loose. They spent a few mags into the bushes where it came from. Amazingly, none of our guys were hurt.

As the first rounds were hitting the building, Pete C., a Rhodesian, was the first one on the scene. Now, Pete is something else. Picture a 62-year-old bloke, long unkept grey hair, Skinny as hell, scraggy beard, no teeth for most of the time but tough as nails. He was special forces back in the day, in the Scouts like Gerry. He's got this fantastic but weird sense of humour – when surprised about something his saying is 'Well, fuck my big black dog' . . . and the laugh, an unusual sound to say the least!

So, as the bullets start flying, Pete runs up to the roof in nothing but his brown Y-fronts, not a care in the world. One of the lads shouted at him, 'Curly, where's your boots?!' Without missing a beat, Pete yells back, 'Fuck my boots, get my teeth!' Turns out, in all the commotion, someone had kicked his choppers across the floor. Priorities, right?

Thankfully, no one was injured, and this was just an opportunity attack, someone checking out our security perhaps.

It was absolute bedlam, but at least we can have a laugh about it now. It's crazy how, in the middle of all this madness, moments like that can bring a bit of levity. Even on Christmas Day, with gunfire echoing in the distance, we find some humour in the chaos.

A couple of hours have passed and I'm now getting the chance to wish the family Merry Xmas. I'm on Skype watching Kyle opening his presents, he's still half asleep and it looks magical back home, the snow has come and has settled outside, and the house looks so cosy and warm.

Kyle is in his pyjamas with his hair all messy and his eyes filled with wonder. I'm telling him how much I miss him and love him, and I'll be home soon, he's too distracted opening his presents though. He told me I would get my presents when I came home. Just coming home will be the gift I'm thinking. The pay is great out here and I can't wait to spoil everyone when I get back, may even spoil myself a bit. Sarah has a look of warmth in her eyes, but I can tell she's finding this difficult too. I say my goodbyes and wish them a happy Xmas and hope they have a good day under the circumstances.

The local guards have done us a Christmas dinner, they went to the market and bought a sheep's head, yip, a fucking sheep's head! Boiled it up with some veg and hay presto! A meal fit for a king. I passed on that shit and had a ration pack!

Sunday 28 December 2003

It had been quiet for a while, but that didn't last long. Yesterday, two of our teams were hit hard, and things have escalated. Intelligence is pointing the finger at the Fedayeen, Saddam's paramilitary force. The first ambush happened in Baghdad. One of the teams was travelling along a stretch of road when a shepherd decided to cross with his herd of sheep. The second vehicle had to come to a stop, and that's when all hell broke loose. Armed fuckers hit them from behind.

One of the internationals who got caught in the ambush was a close mate of Gerry's, Pete Curley, the Rhodesian I've mentioned before. The driver and the rear guard didn't stand a chance; they were killed instantly in the gunfire due to the soft skin vehicles. Pete, miraculously, was still alive at that point. But as the driver died, his foot jammed down on the accelerator, and the car veered off the road into a deep river. The vehicle sank almost immediately.

Pete described what happened next, and it's horrifying. The windows were electrical, and the doors had central locking, so he couldn't get them open. He was trapped inside, with the bodies of the driver and rear guard floating above him, pushing him down. He couldn't escape. He said he'd accepted his fate at that moment, said goodbye to his wife and kids in his mind and started to die. Then, by some miracle, he found himself floating out through the back window, which had been shot out.

When he reached the surface, some local Iraqis spotted him and dragged him out of the river. They rushed him to the nearest hospital. Pete's been through a lot in his life, he's no stranger to danger, but he admitted that this time, he was absolutely terrified. And to top it off, he lost his bloody teeth again!

Pete's been pretty shaken up by the whole thing. He was getting a swimming pool built at his house in South Africa, but after this, he called his wife and told her to seal it up. He's in bad shape, physically and mentally. What he went through is enough to mess anyone up.

Wednesday 31 December 2003 (Hogmanay)

Back in Baghdad for a couple of days, and it's shaping up to be an odd end to the year. We had to bring up a Moroccan prisoner to escort out of the country. This lying bastard had bluffed his way into the company, claiming he'd served in the French Foreign Legion. Turns out, he was in absolutely nothing, no training, no background, just a normal young guy who was looking for adventure, he just spun a story and hoped it would stick. This happens more than you'd think in this industry. Some blokes watch a couple of action films, maybe do a quick 'Weekend course', and suddenly they reckon they're ready for the front lines. The harsh reality out here, though, is that they are found out quickly. And once they do, they're shunned, or worse, they get a good kicking from the lads. These imposters don't just risk their own necks, they risk ours, and that's unacceptable.

On the way up to Baghdad, we had to make an unscheduled stop in Al Amarah because one of the vehicles started spewing out smoke. We pulled into our camp there, and when the guys heard we were escorting a prisoner, they were straight to the point. 'Lock him in a room,' they told me, 'And if he so much as opens his mouth, beat the shit out of him.'

We finally got into Baghdad around midday after the locals fixed our vehicle with a coat hanger and a roll of duct tape. The Baghdad boys were there to greet us, and Gerry immediately spotted his old mate Pete, the one who survived that brutal ambush on the 28th.

Pete's a shadow of the man he used to be. He's been through hell. He was shaking like a leaf, hands trembling uncontrollably as he retold the story of that day, going over every detail like it was stuck on repeat in his mind. The guy's tough, no doubt about it, but that experience has rattled him to his core. Seeing him like that, I couldn't help but feel sorry for him. This place breaks even the hardest of men.

It's a strange Hogmanay, that's for sure. No fireworks, no parties, just the constant undercurrent of danger and the weariness that comes with it.

Gerry and I decided to have a quiet beer and a bite to eat in the Palestine Hotel, trying to unwind after another long, tense day. The place wasn't far from our secure hotel, maybe 200 yards at most. We downed a couple of pints and a quick bite to eat then left. Just as we got back to our complex out of nowhere, 'BOOM!' The whole ground shook. The place we'd just been sitting in, hit by a car bomb!

We could hear people screaming and smoke filled the air. We just looked at each other and said, Fuck me that was close eh! We later learned that seventeen people had been killed in that explosion. Brits, Europeans, civilians, just gone. You go from having a drink, trying to forget for a while, to realising how close you came to being one of the dead. A matter of timing.

I usually don't mind Baghdad. There's something about the city that, despite all the madness, makes it bearable. But tonight, it feels different. Something's off. I feel uncomfortable, like there's a shadow over everything, and I can't shake it. Can't stop thinking about how close we came. I keep thinking about my wife and son back home.

What if I don't make it back? What if something happens, and I'm just another name on the casualty list? My son would grow up without a dad, and that thought's enough to mess with your head. But I have to shove those thoughts deep down. If I let them take over, I won't last long out here. This place demands focus, there's no room for doubts or distractions.

We're staying here in Baghdad for a few more days. The city's a powder keg right now. Last night alone, there were twenty-five separate attacks, and seventeen of them specifically targeted Westerners. It feels like we're being hunted, and every night, you go to bed wondering if you'll be the next target.

Tomorrow we're taking poor Pete back down with us to Basra, his mental state is shot to fuck, he's had enough, called it a day and heading back to South Africa.

Monday 5 January 2004

After months in this place, I'm finally getting some leave in a few days. I can't wait to get home, but there's a part of me that's reluctant to leave the team behind. Over time, the locals I've worked with have become more than just allies, they've become mates, we've been through some demanding times and that builds a bond you don't break easily. They will get a new Team Leader when I'm away and They're pissed off, and honestly, I feel the same.

Out here, it's not just about doing your job. It's about survival. Every man watches the other's back because that's the only way you make it out. It's something that people back home won't understand. The camaraderie out here is different, it's deeper, forged through shared danger and trust. It becomes like family, and stepping away from that, even for a bit of leave, feels harder than you'd expect.

Sure, I'm looking forward to seeing my family, back to a nice bed and decent food, but I'll miss the team, the routine, and the unspoken bond.

The company has just rented some new vehicles for us, they are still soft skins but are really nice shiny Mitsubishi Shoguns, lovely bits of kit and at least this time they won't pack in on longer journeys.

Before my leave though, it's business as usual, yet again, we've been tasked to head back up to Baghdad. Apparently, HQ reckons we're the go-to crew because we actually like the place. Either that or they're secretly hoping we'll get lost and never come back.

Gerry and I were thinking about the absolutely shite handheld radios we've been lumbered with. Honestly, two cans on a piece of string would probably be an upgrade. So, since we're covering long distances, we figured we should try to blag some decent fitted sets for the vehicles.

While killing time at Airport Camp, we decided on a wee nosy around, purely professional reconnaissance, of course. Lo and behold, we stumble into an Aladdin's cave of comms kit. Fuck it, Gerry says, grabbing a set and antenna. Might as well requisition a couple, the lads there obviously didn't need them, or they wouldn't have left the door unlocked, right?

Back at our villa, we get stuck into the delicate installation procedure, two idiots drilling holes in brand-new rented Shoguns. There's me hanging off the roof like a pissed orangutan, Gerry shouting directions like a deaf foreman, bits of plastic flying everywhere. Honestly, if Hertz rentals saw us now, they'd have a bloody stroke.

Finally, we wire everything up, flick the switches, hold our breath and . . . fuck all. Well, technically they switched on, but they're about as useful as tits on a fish without the right codes.

And as if on cue, the boss rocks up to witness our handy work. One look at the fresh holes in his shiny new jeeps, and his face turns a special shade of purple.

Thursday 8 January 2004

Last night, we rolled into Baghdad. The mission was to escort three flatbed trucks. We stayed in a nice secure hotel, which was great, hot water, clean sheets, the works. A bit of luxury before diving back into the madness. It's the little things that make me happy.

Come morning, Gerry got this wild idea around 0530hrs and decided to wake me up. 'Let's go out for a spin,' he said. 'Just you and me, no team, Let's do a recce on our own. It'll help us learn the streets.' I didn't argue. So, there we were, both in our nice new Shoguns, driving around Baghdad like a couple of nutters, just two blokes with an AK each sitting in the footwell and a radio to keep in touch. Baghdad at dawn is something else, eerily quiet, almost peaceful if you didn't know what it could become in a heartbeat. But it's a different kind of quiet, strange experience.

We were the only cars on the road, which is never a good sign. The streets were deserted, not a soul in sight, apart from the occasional corpse, sprawled in the middle of the road. Local police officers dragged the bodies away like it was just another day, trying to clear the streets before the city erupted again in its usual chaos. It was surreal, but that's Baghdad!

The other guys thought we'd lost it, driving around like that. No one in their right mind goes out at that hour, but Gerry wanted to get a feel for the city, and I wasn't going to sit it out. There's something about the place that gets under your skin, and before you know it, you're doing things that would seem insane anywhere else.

Later, we set off from Baghdad back to Basra, knowing full well that we'd be hitting 'Ambush Alley' after dark. That stretch between Al Amarah and Qurna is notorious, especially at night. The bastard militia just sit and wait for you at the side of the road, ready to hit you when you're most vulnerable.

The drive was smooth enough for most of the trip, but as soon as we got near the alley, things went sideways. Gerry was leading the convoy, and over the radio, he called in: 'Suspect vehicles ahead. Two Toyota pickups, lights off.' That was all I needed to hear. We knew these were local militia, they ambush you, take everything, and leave you dead in the dirt. As we passed them, their lights flicked on, and they started tailing us, I knew this was about to get ugly.

I radioed Gerry, told him I was ready to open fire if they got too close. Rambo, sitting in the back, me in the front with my driver. I held my AK out the passenger window, Rambo ready in the back to engage on my command. The next moment, we saw the bastards lean out of their windows with AKs, I gave the word.

We opened up, firing bursts straight from the vehicles. The air filled with burning shell casings flying back into the car as we let rip. We put about thirty rounds into the first pickup, hitting it hard. The vehicle swerved off the road and crashed into a ditch. The second pickup hesitated but decided to bug out, stopping for his mate. I'm pretty sure we slotted the driver of the first one, but there was no time to check. We weren't about to stop and have a look.

We kept pushing forward, driving another 5km before pulling over to assess what just went down. We both agreed to keep quiet, no point involving the local police. They're as crooked as the militia and trusting them could get us killed just as easily. We gave a report to the boss back in camp , and he did the necessary paperwork. Gerry was fuming that we didn't stop to take trophies, he wanted to cut their ears off as a reminder, I wasn't sure if he was joking or really meant it?

Wednesday 11 February 2004

Sam and I were finally going on leave for a bit, leaving Basra and heading up to Baghdad to catch a military flight out to Amman, Jordan. We started early, but I had a bad feeling this wasn't going to be smooth sailing. We had two older vehicles, and things went wrong when we hit Al Amarah. One of the cars breaks down, leaving us with just the one vehicle for the rest of the journey. Now we're all crammed in together, no backup, and crucially, no rear gunner, pretty much a sitting target.

By the time we hit Baghdad, it was already getting dark. Nightfall in Baghdad means everyone with a grudge or an AK is out hunting. We managed to contact HQ on the VHF, and they sent a vehicle with some guys to meet us. Relief, right? Wrong. The crew they sent were new, and sure enough, the driver gets lost. Now we're sitting ducks in the centre of Baghdad, in some dodgy, dark street, trying to get directions back to base.

Sam and I were pissed off, we knew staying there was a terrible idea, but the new guys weren't listening. The longer we stayed, the worse it got. We heard shouting in the distance, then the unmistakable sound of weapons being cocked. Bollox to this, get in the cars and let's get the fuck out of here before we end up in a firefight the night before going home.

We finally made it to base, but the whole crew was *threaders*. After that near-miss, I figured I'd had enough of these escorts and took matters into my own hands. I knew Baghdad pretty well by now and decided to head to a secure hotel we'd used before. We ditched the escort, figuring we could handle it.

Picture this – an Iraqi vehicle, an Iraqi driver, Sam in the back, and me up front. All of us armed to the teeth with AKs and shemaghs covering our faces. Normally, we carry our standard flash cards to Identify us to coalition, but not this time.

As we turn a corner in pitch black, we didn't notice the Humvee tucked off the side of the road. But they saw us. Suddenly, I spotted the red dot of a laser sight sweep over our vehicle and zero in on my chest. FUCK! Sam shouted. Without thinking, I tossed my weapon into the footwell and ducked. The top gunner must've had night vision, but as we were going round a bend, he couldn't get a clean shot. By some miracle, we slipped away.

We just burned through another one of our nine lives.

On Leave

I'm back home now, I have a few weeks home before I'm due to head back out. First thing I did was book a proper holiday for the family. If I've only got three weeks, I'm going to make them count. One of the few perks of working in Iraq is the money. It's fantastic. At least I don't have to stress about bills or counting pennies while I'm on leave.

That said, even though I'm home, I don't feel fully here. My body's back, but my head's still out there, still wired. I catch myself wandering around in cargo trousers and an old Under Armour t-shirt like I'm about to jump into an SUV and roll out on task. Sarah keeps having a go, 'Can you not just wear something normal for once?' she says. Maybe throw on a proper shirt, ditch the desert boots. I get it. She wants her husband back, not some dust, covered contractor stuck in war, mode. But for me, the 5.11s and boots are more than just clothes. They're like a second skin now. Familiar. Practical. Safe.

Our rotations are tough, eight to twelve weeks in-country, then only three weeks at home. Three weeks to switch off, reconnect, and pretend this life is normal. But the time just vanishes. So, I make sure every spare second I have, is with Kyle. Him and I are thick as thieves when I'm home. Day trips, ice cream runs, holidays, whatever he wants, even when he doesn't ask. I just want to make memories while I can. Life is so fragile. And that wee lad – he's my world. I record all the laughs, the silly things he does, that happy wee face, all imprinted in my memory bank.

This break's been something else, a couple of weeks in a plush all-inclusive in Portugal. Best part's getting up before the sun, wandering down to the beach while it's still quiet. Coffee in one hand, smokes in the other, I'll sit there and listen to the sea roll in. Just me, the sound of the waves, and my own thoughts. The world feels lighter in those moments. You realise how lucky you are to be here, with the people you love, watching another day begin.

Chapter 4

Back In

Monday 1 March 2004

I've been back on the ground here for two weeks now after a great leave with the family, but the last four days have been rough. The local food's done a number on me, had me sick as a dog. Spent two days straight down for the count, barely moving. Once I got past that, things have been relatively quiet for us.

Only two incidents worth noting this past week: both were drive-by shootings, and we had some incoming RPK fire hitting the compound. Our exterior guard force dealt with it swiftly, putting up a good fight. The most surreal moment though, being jolted awake at 0200 hours by the rattle of heavy machine gun fire right outside your window. Heart's racing, adrenaline kicks in, and for a few seconds, it feels like you're stuck between reality and some kind of dream. But you shake it off fast when you remember you're in a war zone, not back home and try and get some shut eye.

I've got a new posting for the next couple of weeks, billeted with the British Army down in Khowr Az Zubayr, south of Basra. Tasked with providing protection for two Perini bosses who are based inside the camp. The routine is simple: we collect the principals around 0700 hours, hit the cookhouse for breakfast, then head over to the power station at 0800. The site's only 4km away, so not a long haul.

There's just three of us on this detail, my good pal Bob, Ian and big Jack. Jack is the gaffer here, a posh lad from London. We've got our own office at the power station. It's air-conditioned, which is a godsend in this heat. Plus, we've got two computers with internet access, so that's a bonus. Honestly, this has been the easiest assignment so far. If I'm being honest, it's almost too easy, it borders on boring.

The power station's locked down tight, with local Iraqi guards securing both the perimeter and the inside. Our two VIPs are stationed in the connex next to ours, so they're close by and easy to manage. We head back to base around midday for lunch at the camp and wrap things up by 1600, 1700 hours. After that, it's back to the tented city, gym, shower, and maybe catch a movie to kill time.

I still can't believe I'm getting paid for this gig, compared to the high, risk stuff up north, this feels like a holiday. But we all know the calm never lasts long out here.

Sunday 7 March 2004

Today has been an absolute shit show. I called HQ in Basra to get the latest Intel and check in on what's happening on the ground. That's when Hamish, the PM, drops a bombshell on me, he's had to fire Gerry, my oppo. I couldn't believe what I was hearing.

Straight after, I gave Gerry a call, and the moment he picked up, I could tell he was in a bad way. His voice was wrecked, like a man who's been beaten down. Turns out he got completely pissed, went on a bender, and ended up missing his mission the next morning. I can't say I've ever seen Gerry like this before. I used to keep an eye on him, always making sure the big man wasn't hitting the booze too hard. When we were together, I kept him busy, kept him focused. But ever since our team got split, it's like he's given up, like something inside him just broke.

I wasn't aware, but Gerry is convinced the project manager has had it in for him for a while now. Gerry thinks he should've been the one in his position, running the show down here. He's been harbouring that resentment for a bit it seems, but I didn't realise it was eating away at him this much. Now, with the split and everything else, it feels like he's spiralled.

Talking to him on the phone was hard. I've never heard Gerry sound so lost. For a man his size, physically and in presence, hearing him ashamed and broken like that was shit. He's always been the big man, the reliable one, but now? He's a shadow of who he used to be. He's stuck in this deep pit of self-loathing, and I can't help but feel like I failed him by not being there when he needed someone to pull him back from the edge.

He's flying back home tomorrow, I'm sure I will see him back out with another company soon though. I will miss him, but at least he's not going home in a box.

Around 1600hrs today, I received more devastating news: Neil Cameron had been killed in a road traffic accident. Neil and I arrived in Iraq together from day one, and we had known each other for a few years before that from Edinburgh.

According to HQ, Neil's car was completely wrecked in the accident. Two Iraqi passengers were critically injured, and Neil was pronounced dead at the scene. His body is being sent to Kuwait. Ian Watt, one of the company's senior managers who lives in Edinburgh, is tasked with breaking the news to Neil's girlfriend tonight. I can't even begin to imagine what that conversation will be like.

That night, as I was sleeping, I ended up having a strange dream. I walked into HQ, and there was Neil, sitting right next to me. I said, 'Shit, you look good for a dead man,' and he replied, 'They made a mistake. Thought I was dead and left me, but I wasn't.' I remember feeling a surge of relief as we shook hands in the dream. But when I woke up, the harsh reality hit me, he was gone. It's shit, especially since just two days ago, Neil had jokingly said we were more likely to die in a car crash out here than in a firefight. I laughed it off and told him he was a jinx with cars, referencing the time we almost died coming into country and the time had to go home in October for R&R after totalling another vehicle in Baghdad. Now, his words seem hauntingly prophetic. It's a harsh and unforgiving world out here.

Today, I got the full details on Neil's death. He was escorting a convoy up to Nasiriyah during a severe sandstorm. Neil had instructed his driver to overtake a line of vehicles, not realising an Iraqi arctic was coming head, on. The collision was catastrophic, and Neil died almost instantly. They airlifted him to an American hospital, but he was declared dead on arrival.

Ian Watt went to deliver the news to Neil's girlfriend, Wendy. Her initial reaction was one of disbelief; she burst out laughing, thinking it was a cruel joke. 'Okay, tell Neil he's a shit for playing jokes on me,' she said. It took Ian several attempts to convince her of the tragic reality before she finally accepted it.

I also spoke with Sarah today. Another friend of mine, Joe has arrived in country with us on another contract, and he and his wife have set up a grim but necessary agreement with mine. If something happens to me, Christine will go to our house to break the news to Sarah. Conversely, if Joe were to die, my wife would do the same for Christine. It's a tough arrangement, but it's better coming from someone you know.

Thursday 18 March 2004

I've been in Iraq for just over a month now, on my second tour. Things have been intense, but last night was the first time I had a nightmare in ages. I dreamt about bleeding to death after being blown up. It's unsettling how the mind processes the stress out here.

I'm still stationed at the Khor Az Zubayr power station. Living at the British camp has its perks, good food and decent living conditions. However, the situation outside is anything but calm. Last night, there was a massive explosion in Baghdad. Reports suggest another hotel has been obliterated. It's becoming hard to keep track of the damage; there can't be many hotels left?

We got back to camp after a day's work to hear about a car bomb detonating outside our original hotel in Basra, the Mirbad. We all knew it was only a matter of time before the hotel was hit. Thankfully, our team had been pulled out in time, The attack, claimed by Al-Qaeda, resulted in the deaths of four Iraqis. What didn't make the news was that the local Iraqi population caught three of the bombers and executed them by kicking them to death. It's a brutal form of justice, but it seems to fit the context.

Tuesday 23 March 2004

Yesterday, Bob and I made a run to Shaibah Military Camp, which is about a 20-minute drive from camp. We were supposed to pick up some beer and cigarettes, but we took a wrong turn that led us into Al Zubayr town. This area is notorious, controlled by Shia militia and a local cleric. It looked like a scene from *Black Hawk Down*. The streets were packed with locals, and the kids were hurling insults and stones at us.

We decided it was best to get out before things escalated further. On the way back to base, I was driving, and I noticed we were being followed by two high-speed vehicles. Bob, in a moment of high tension, drew his AK and yelled at them, 'Come on ya fuckers' I was right there with him, urging him to shoot if they got any closer. Fortunately, the vehicles backed off before it came to a firefight.

Back at the base, things were chaotic. There were mass riots in Basrah's centre as hundreds of Iraqis protested over job shortages, blaming the coalition forces for their plight. The riots turned violent, with petrol bombs being thrown at our troops. It was a grim scene, and the injuries sustained by 13 soldiers, including three from our camp, highlighted just how volatile the situation is. It's frustrating that the response here is limited to tear gas, especially when the Americans would likely handle it with more force. Sometimes it feels like we're just trying to keep the peace with one hand tied behind our backs.

The latest report on TV has got us all wound up……

> BAGHDAD, Iraq. Four civilian contractors who worked for Blackwater USA of Moyock, N.C., and five US troops were killed today in one of the bloodiest and most horrifying days since the end of the US, led war in Iraq, MSNBC News has reported. After an ambush on two vehicles carrying the civilians in Falluja, jubilant Iraqis burned and mutilated the dead, then dragged two corpses through the streets and hung them from a bridge spanning the Euphrates River.
>
> The brutal treatment of the bodies occurred after the contractors were killed in a rebel attack on their two SUVs in the city about 35 miles west of Baghdad, scene of some of the worst violence on both sides of the conflict since the beginning of the American occupation a year ago. According to MSNBC, Brig. Gen. Mark Kimmitt said at a briefing in Baghdad that it was not known what the coalition contractors were doing in Fallujah , apparently without a military escort, when the attack occurred. officials, who spoke with NBC News on condition of anonymity, said that all four contractors were Americans who worked for Blackwater USA of Moyock, N.C.

These individuals were engaged in the same operations as us here in Iraq, but what happened recently marks a significant escalation. For the first time, the anger and frustration among the local population have manifested in such a violent and public manner. The streets have become battlegrounds, with rioting and attacks becoming more brazen and ruthless.

The intensity of the violence is a stark reminder that we are now a primary target. The local insurgents and hostile factions are no longer just indirect threats; they are actively seeking us out, viewing us as the enemy in their struggle. This shift in the dynamics of the conflict has heightened our sense of vulnerability and underscores the harsh reality that we are directly in the line of fire. It's not just a matter of being in a dangerous environment; we are now explicitly marked as adversaries by those who are escalating their aggression against us. This new level of hostility brings with it an increased urgency to remain vigilant and prepared for any potential attack.

Tuesday 6 April 2004

Yesterday was a total clusterfuck. The entire situation unravelled into chaos. Two influential clerics, one from Basra and one from Baghdad, took to the airwaves and declared a holy war against the coalition forces, calling on the people to rise up and fight as an act of divine will. The result was immediate and catastrophic.

The first reports hit us with Baghdad being hit hard, followed quickly by Fallujah, Al, Amara, Nasiriya, and finally Basra. It was an all-out uprising. We received an urgent call to evacuate the power station as militias were reportedly heading our way with intentions to kill us all. We quickly deployed our guards and briefed the clients on the situation, advising them that we had to evacuate immediately.

One of our American principals, who had served in Vietnam, was visibly shaken by the unfolding events. The reality of the situation hit him hard. As we made our way to the military camp, it was clear that a lockdown was our only option. HQ contacted us with the directive that all our positions had been evacuated and that we were restricted to base with no permission to move outside.

What a bummer! We had plans to visit the US Camp for smokes and beer, but instead we found ourselves sitting outside our tent, making the best of it with a bit of sunbathing. I'm heading over to Kuwait tomorrow for a bit of leave at home so better get some rays before I go.

Wednesday 7 April 2004 1700hrs

I'm now in Kuwait with some lads waiting for our flight home for leave, but we've just received some dire news from HQ. Our team in Al Kut is currently surrounded by local militia and taking intense incoming fire. The situation is grim, there are only five of them left, and they're fighting to hold their ground as best they can. We're in constant communication with HQ, and one of the guys on the roof has a phone link, so we're getting regular situation reports.

I've just been informed that one of our men, Grey Branfield, has been shot. He's taken a round in the leg and another in the gut. The bastards have breached the house, and the team has been forced to retreat to the roof. Grey, however, is badly wounded and remains downstairs. The Ukrainian army, stationed only 15 minutes away, was supposed to be the quick reaction force, but Uri, who is here with us waiting to go on leave too, speaks Ukrainian and is reporting that they're too busy to assist. So, our guys are left to fend for themselves.

2300hrs

Six hours have passed, and the fight continues. Our men are still pinned on the roof. Every time the lads try to go down and attempt to reach Grey, the militia opens up on them from below. This prolonged battle is taking a serious toll. I reached out to Jack, an ex-officer who's in touch with high, ranking officials at the British camp. They're attempting to mobilise a response from Al Amara, but they won't deploy a chopper for extraction because it would be an easy target for enemy fire. It's infuriating, we would go ourselves if we could.

0100hrs – 8 hours later

The fight is still ongoing, and no help has arrived. It's with a heavy heart that I've learned Grey Branfield has died. The situation is beyond frustrating. We're powerless to intervene, and our comrades are left to battle alone against overwhelming odds.

Every time I'm back on leave, I can't help thinking about the lads who didn't get the chance. The ones who never made it home. I sit there at the dinner table with Sarah and Kyle, smiling, nodding at whatever the conversation's about, but in the back of my head, I'm seeing the faces of the lads. Their faces stay with me. Some I knew well. Some I barely had time to learn their names. But they all bleed into the same memory, good lads who just wanted to do the job and get home safe. They didn't get the second chance I've had.

I catch myself planning the future like I've got it all mapped out, talking about next year, thinking about where to put money, maybe moving house. But it all feels fragile. Like I'm tempting fate. Because deep down, I know the odds. I know that every time I step off that plane and land back in country, I'm spinning the barrel again.

When I first signed up for this, it was meant to be four months. Quick hit. Make a decent chunk of cash, stash it away, and figure out the next move. I told myself it was just a stop gap, something to bridge the gap between gigs. But that was six months ago. And now? I can't see myself walking away from it.

This work, it's in me now. The tempo, the purpose, the way everything matters out there. I've been in the civvy CP game for over six years, bouncing from one job to the next, keeping people safe here in Europe and in the UK But Iraq? This is different. This is raw. Real. Life and death in every single decision. There's no safety net. No back, up plan. You're either switched on, or you're not coming home.

And as brutal as it is . . . it suits me. I feel alive out there. Clear. Like I've found the one thing I was meant to do. Maybe that's fucked up. But all I know is, that place, the dust, the danger, the noise, it makes sense in a way that nothing home does.

I'd volunteered to head back to Basra, hoping for a bit more action, couldn't sit twiddling my thumbs much longer in the power station.

We'd all packed up and left the houses in town, moved into this old Global camp inside Basra Airport. It's a bit of a mixed bag, Brits are here, the Danes have their own patch, there's a NAAFI, some shops, even a bar called the TUKAN (two can limit) that pretends to serve cold beer.

Living arrangements are cosy, four blokes in long white cabins with soft roofs, ringed by sandbags that have seen better days. Each one's got air-con and a TV/DVD setup, which is great for watching all the pirate copy movies the locals sell.

Main thing that keeps you on edge here is the mortars and rockets. We've got a C-RAM Phalanx on base, it's basically R2 D2 with a minigun, it tracks incoming with radar and fills the sky with hot metal. It looks like something from Star Wars and sounds like the world's angriest dentist. It does a decent job, but the odd one still gets through. Still, I'd take my chances here over the houses in town.

Saturday 15 May 2004

We had a mission to haul four big trucks to Buzurgan, right on the Iranian border. We had to navigate through Al Amarah, which was a hotbed of trouble. Al Amarah was in total lockdown at this time, so we asked for a military escort. We met up with the Brits just outside town, a soft skin Land Rover and a Saracen APC. We were meant to have two Warrior tanks to get us through, but they were called away to an incident. Our formation was the brit land rover then our four vehicles up front, four trucks in the middle, four vehicles bringing up the rear, and the Saracen closing the convoy. The town was eerily quiet, no kids playing, nothing, that's the first combat indicator that things are way off.

The convoy kicked off and immediately we were in the thick of it. A mortar exploded a hundred feet to our right. 'Keep moving, keep moving' came over the radios, though it was clear things were about to get messy. As we approached a sharp bend in the road, more mortars rained down on us. Grenades hit the ground in front of our vehicle, showering us with shrapnel. We were crawling along at about

10 miles per hour, when all hell broke loose. We were hit from both sides of the street from the high, rise buildings by militia armed with AKs. The world slowed down to a crawl everything went in slow motion as I passed the message over the radio, 'CONTACT LEFT – CONTACT LEFT!'

Everyone hung out of the vehicles and opened up, laying down heavy fire. It wasn't long before we heard, 'CONTACT RIGHT!' Picture this: eight security vehicles, each with four operators, all firing AKs out of the windows or out behind concrete cover, while the Saracen APC hammered the buildings with its heavy GPMG. The noise was deafening, and I was right in the thick of it, blasting into the buildings, laying down suppressive fire. We couldn't even see the enemy; they were well, hidden in doorways, opened windows and rooftops.

As I was firing into on a window where a gunman was intermittently popping up and down, I saw something that will forever haunt my nightmares. Amidst the chaos, a young girl, perhaps ten or eleven years old, was thrust into my line of fire by the gunman. She wore a bright red dress and a black scarf, her tiny hands frantically trying to cover her ears against the enormity of gunfire. She emerged abruptly, right in my line of sight. In the frantic moments of the firefight, I mistook her for a threat and didn't manage to stop in time.

The impact of the rounds was instantaneous. The rounds bursting into the window and the concrete flying around it and I saw her small frame drop, and time seemed to freeze for a heartbeat. The reality of what had just happened hit me like a sledgehammer. I was overwhelmed with a sense of dread and guilt so profound it nearly paralysed me. Had I just taken an innocent life amidst the chaos of battle?

I had no choice but to force myself back into the fight. Each burst of fire felt like an assault on my own sanity, but the urgency to survive and protect those around me pushed me forward. I was engulfed in a turmoil of guilt and shock, struggling to reconcile the horrors of war with the weight of what I had done.

Have I just killed a kid? The weight of it was crushing, but we couldn't afford to stop. If I had taken her life, I could only plead for forgiveness from above. Despite the traumatic sight, I had to pull myself together and rejoin the fight.

The enemy clearly wasn't prepared for the level of retaliation we unleashed. We managed to neutralise several of them and push through.

After we had driven out of the kill zone, we stopped to regroup and assess the situation. Remarkably, the vehicles had only sustained minor damage, and there were no casualties. It felt like someone was looking out for us, given the sheer luck of our survival.

Tuesday 18 May 2004

It's been two days since the firefight, and I can't shake the image of that little girl from my mind. Every time I close my eyes, I see her face, and it haunts me. She was so young, I can't help but feel an overwhelming sense of anger and sadness. Anger that she wasn't protected by those who should have kept her safe, and sadness for the life she was forced to live in such a brutal place.

I'm struggling to sleep, the nightmares are relentless, and I'm questioning everything. I keep thinking about how I could have done something differently, how I could have prevented her death. The weight of it all is suffocating. I miss home, miss my family, and the longing to escape this nightmare is unbearable.

I called Sarah, my voice cracking as I tried to explain how I'm feeling. I'm overwhelmed, and I feel like I'm losing my grip. I need someone to tell me it wasn't my fault, that there was nothing more I could have done. The guilt is eating me alive.

'Scott…' she said quietly, steady but not cold. 'You were ambushed. It is a war zone, not some controlled environment where you get to stop and think. You reacted in the middle of chaos – split seconds, gunfire, survival. No one back here can fully understand what that means. But I know you. And I know you didn't go expecting this . .'

'You've always carried more than your share. But this . . . this wasn't your fault. You didn't choose that situation, the bastard that was meant to be protecting this kid did this. And in the middle of al the madness, something tragic happened, something that never should've happened. But that doesn't make you a bad man. It makes you human in a place where humanity is torn to pieces.'

She let out a breath. 'This is hurting you, I know that, but you need to get your head back in the game and when you come home, we'll face it together, one day at a time. You don't have to carry all of it on your own.'

It's been a week after the incident in Al Amarah, and we're sent back up that way again.

We were heading back from the Iranian border with two trucks and a client from Perini. Everything was going smoothly until one of the truck's tires blew out. We all debussed and set up a perimeter around the disabled vehicles.

While we were securing the area, two white pickups pulled up about 100m away. This was typical; the locals often wait for a vehicle to break down, then move in to attack. I ordered my team to stand by, keeping a watchful eye on the pickups.

Suddenly – BANG! – a shot rang out. I spun around to find one of my Iraqi guards standing there, his face contorted in shock and embarrassment. He had accidentally discharged his weapon in front of the client. The situation was bad enough without adding this kind of mistake into the mix.

I walked over to him, quickly clearing his weapon and gave him a look that he knew wasn't good. He was visibly shaken and started to cry. He pleaded with me in broken English, his voice cracking as he told me he had eight children to support and begged for any help he could get. I felt a pang of guilt and sympathy; Kadham was a good man, always smiling and doing his best despite the harsh conditions.

But rules are rules. He knew what was about to happen, I had no choice, I had to take him to my boss, and the decision was final. It was heart, wrenching to see him break down, repeatedly apologising as if he could somehow undo the mistake. If he didn't do it in front of the client, I may have been able to keep quiet. But there was no way I could have hid this.

Before he left, I slipped $200 into his hand. It wasn't much, but it was something. I told him how sorry I was and that I wished things could be different. The look of gratitude and despair in his eyes was almost too much to bear.

I walked away feeling like a failure, burdened by the weight of rules that felt so cold and unforgiving. Kadham had been a good man, and now, because of one mistake, his livelihood and dignity were taken from him.

Monday 21 June 2004

Only nine days remain before the official handover of Basra to the Iraqi authorities. The atmosphere here is thick with uncertainty. Predictions of civil war are rampant, and it seems almost inevitable that the situation will deteriorate. The quiet that has settled over the area in the past few days feels ominous, like the calm before a storm. Locals are whispering that all militia groups are amassing more personnel and weapons in preparation for 30 June. My scheduled departure for leave is on 4 July, Independence Day, but with the growing instability, I'm increasingly doubtful about making it out on time.

This morning, we received an intelligence report that paints a grim picture of what's to come:

Intelligence Report:
Mullah Mahmood Al-Hassani is leading a new anti-Iraq faction called Ansar Al-Mehdi. Operating out of Najaf, Nasiriyah, and Basra, this group is estimated to consist of

approximately 300 fighters. Al-Hassani positions himself as the supreme leader of Muslims and seeks to subvert the Iraqi government by sowing chaos. The group is expected to target government officials, high, profile personalities, and critical infrastructure, including multi, national forces.

Furthermore, the arrival of 200 Chechen fighters in Iraq was confirmed on the 16th of June. These Chechens are seasoned terrorists with expertise in making and deploying IEDs. Their proficiency in guerrilla tactics and urban warfare poses an even greater threat if they are linked with foreign fighters in the region.

Monday 28 June 2004

In a surprising move, Iraqi Prime Minister Allawi, in coordination with the Americans, has decided to transfer sovereignty to the Iraqi government today, two days ahead of the official handover date. The decision is a tactical one, intended to catch insurgents off guard who were planning major attacks on military bases, civilian targets, and government properties on the 30th. Our team has been rigorously training for this scenario, setting up new shelters and refining our SOP's. However, we face a significant challenge: when the attacks come, and they will, it won't just be a single mortar round. The insurgents will likely use multiple rockets, and with us living in porta cabins that offer no protection, the shrapnel could easily cause serious casualties.

Today's operations were particularly tense. With the power transition underway, many Iraqis mistakenly believe that coalition forces will no longer engage if provoked. This misunderstanding could make our job even more perilous.

At 1400 hours, we proceeded to the Kuwait/Iraq border to do a drop off. As we arrived, we noticed we were being followed by a white car with tinted windows. After parking in a makeshift car park on the Iraqi side, we observed four more vehicles pulling up about 200m away. The occupants of these cars were clearly up to no good, as evidenced by their behaviour and phone conversations.

I gave the orders to my guys to get out the vehicles and get into covering positions. I was in a particularly bad mood today; I decided to confront the situation personally. With my 2ic covering me, I approached one of the vehicles, sticking my weapon through the driver's side window. The occupants were visibly startled, and the driver, in a nervous English accent, bizarrely asked if I had watched the football the previous night.

The fucking football?

Incredulous at the absurdity of his question given the context, I ordered the driver and his two passengers out of the vehicle and onto the ground. I conducted a thorough search of the car and its boot, finding no weapons or explosives. The other vehicles, seeing that we were onto them, quickly fucked off. Were they a scout vehicle preparing a firing team from the others?

Our mission was to escort trucks from the border to the base, but I decided against risking my team's safety for a cargo that seemed less crucial compared to the potential threat. The Americans informed us that local militia had planned to attack coalition vehicles at the border, confirming that our instincts had been right.

I reported the incident and made the decision to withdraw and return to base. The instability here is palpable.

I've been given a new team here, with a new set of blokes, which means I've got to start from scratch with training and building bonds. My second-in-command is Ian, ex SAS guy, decent bloke but no CP experience. My third is Leo, a Frenchman who, to put it mildly, is a bit of a challenge. His arrogance and inability to follow orders are testing my patience. I've requested a replacement for him and hopefully, I'll get someone who at least speaks English fluently.

Basra is currently one of the most perilous places I've seen. We're surrounded by around a thousand militia who are openly displaying their firepower on the streets with rocket launchers and AKs. The situation has restricted our movement severely; we're basically confined to base until things settle down.

In the last two weeks, we've lost six men, and shockingly, most of these casualties were due to the extreme heat – 65°C (149°F). The heat is so intense it melts the tar on the roads and causes tires to blow out at speed. We've had several vehicles roll over because of this. Just yesterday, we had to recover Hammed, a driver whose face was almost completely destroyed and whose hips were twisted backward in the wreck. Another guard was torn in half after being thrown from the vehicle and trapped when it rolled. The heat and the violence are taking a toll that's hard to quantify.

My first few days back have been unnervingly quiet, but only because we can hardly move anywhere. The militia's been handing out flyers telling locals to stay inside and warning that any Westerner caught out will be dealt with, violently. It's like living on a knife's edge. The streets might look calm, but it's that false calm you get before everything kicks off again. One wrong move, one spark, and this place will blow wide open.

It's 0300hrs and I'm on guard duty. Three-hour stags, but given the current threat level, it's necessary. We rotate shifts with one team on duty each night. With seven teams stationed here, the rotation isn't too gruelling, you only find yourself on guard once a week or so.

At this time during the night here, everything is shrouded in darkness. The camp entrance is eerily silent, save for the occasional distant explosion or flare that lights up the horizon. We're positioned about two miles from the city centre at Basra Airport, so while we're far enough to avoid immediate danger, the backdrop of sporadic flashes reminds us of the ongoing chaos. The contrast between the tranquillity of the night sky and the turmoil below is stark.

I find myself staring up at the stars, which seem almost unnaturally bright against the velvet blackness of the sky. It's a breathtaking sight, a reminder of the vastness and beauty of the world. But then I shift my gaze downwards to Basra, where the glow of distant fires and the occasional burst of light from an explosion paint a different, more unsettling picture. It's a surreal position, heavenly stars above, a hellish landscape below. In moments like these, the contrast between peace and conflict feels almost symbolic, a reminder of the fragile boundary between tranquillity and chaos in this part of the world.

Monday 6 September 2004

2100hrs and I just got told I'm heading to Baghdad, Leaving first thing in the morning. I was just in the shower, when one of the project managers here burst in and told me to pack my gear; they need experienced Team Leaders up north for a new contract. I agreed, of course. At the time, it felt like a step forward, another chance to do what I'm trained for.

It's only turned to daylight, my local Iraqi team are in the car park, and I go tell them the news. Adnan my interpreter and now my friend and the rest of the guys were really pushing for me to stay. Their faces said it all, disappointment mixed with a bit of desperation. I couldn't do anything but tell them it wasn't my call.

It's funny how quickly you can get attached. We've been through so much together, and now it feels like I'm leaving behind more than just a job. We've built something solid here, a real team dynamic that's hard to find. I'll miss them, no doubt about it. They have been teaching me Arabic with new words every day and I'm conversing, broken and a bit shit, but I'm trying all the same. They all laugh when I make a mess of it and I just tell them all to shut the fuck up, a good bunch of locals who have put themselves in so much danger to help their country.

Tuesday 7 September 2004

This morning, I boarded a military C-130 for a flight from Basra to Baghdad. The inside of a Hercules is nothing like a commercial plane; it's just a metal shell with netting lining the fuselage. The roar of the engines drowns out any attempt at reading or relaxing without ear defenders, turning the journey into a bone-jarring experience. The take-off is a stomach-churning ascent, with the aircraft climbing sharply to avoid RPGs and rockets. It feels like the fastest rollercoaster you've ever been on. Coming in for landing is just as intense, it's a rapid descent called a combat landing that slams you down, again to minimize exposure to enemy fire.

Now that I'm in Baghdad, it's a different world altogether. The city is unrecognisable from what I remember. Apache gunships circle overhead constantly. I'm part of the new covert operations we're involved in, instead of the usual combat gear, we're blending into the civilian population with plain grey shirts and no visible tactical equipment. I don't even use sunglasses to avoid drawing attention, as they're not commonly worn by locals. To fit in even more, I've donned an occasional Arab outfit, which has been working so well that my suntan might just pass me off as one of them.

Wednesday 8 September 2004

This morning, I was jolted awake at 0400hrs by a loud explosion, followed by a series of mortar rounds. The blasts were close but not direct hits, so I managed to go back to sleep. It's strange how, after months of this, you get accustomed to determining how close mortars land even in your sleep.

By 0700hrs, the situation outside had escalated. Mortars and rockets are still flying past our house, and there's a major firefight going on about 500m away. You can feel the air changing from the explosions, and the noise is constant. From our vantage point on the roof, we can see the intense action around the al-Rashid area, and the constant stream of medical helicopters indicates significant coalition casualties. Apache gunships continue to roar overhead, providing the soundtrack to the chaos.

Our house is located next to the minister of electricity's residence, heavily guarded by the Iraqi INIS (Iraqi National Intelligence Service) and Special Forces. These guards are a constant source of tension; just yesterday, one of them negligently discharged a pistol, nearly hitting one of our lads. If that had escalated, it could have ignited a major punch up. The area is a prime target for insurgents, and we face regular mortar attacks, some of which have been close, down to just meters. It's a daily reminder of the volatile and dangerous environment we're operating in

Tuesday 14 September 2004

We have two local Iraqi housekeepers working in our house/base, Zena and Bushra. Zena is the younger of the two, around 24 years old. She's got a good sense of humour, speaks English well, and is quite pretty by local standards. Normally, she's cheerful, joking around with the guys, but today was different. She was crying, and I could tell something was seriously wrong. I took her outside for a cigarette and asked her what was going on.

She nervously told me that one of our Iraqi guards had put a pistol in her back and threatened to kill her. As she explained further, it transpired she is an informer for the Americans. She'd been spying on one of our key local contacts, the sheikh who's been helping us maintain some resemblance of stability here. This guy isn't just any local figure, though. He's a big player in Falluja and happens to be one of Saddam's cousins.

Everyone here knows who he is and what he's capable of, but we turn a blind eye. He's a necessary evil. Without his protection, we wouldn't be able to operate as freely in Iraq with so few incidents.

His influence ensures that we're in a safer position than many others, and it's no secret that he's paid handsomely for it. In this place, money speaks louder than principles.

However, Zena's double role has put her in grave danger. One of the guards, who is suspected to be part of the Moqtada militia, found out what she's been up to. He knows she's been spying on the sheikh, and that makes her a walking target. She told me she's terrified that her life is at risk, not just from the guards but from anyone who could see her as a traitor. She's worried she won't make it home alive tonight.

I went to speak to our OC, but to my surprise, he wasn't shocked. They already knew about Zena's ties to the Americans. Apparently, she's been in contact with a US sergeant and has even flown with him in a helicopter. They communicate using a burner phone that he gave her. She's shown them a letter that this sergeant wrote to the Iraqi government, requesting permission for her to carry a weapon. The letter even has an official stamp from the American military, which only complicates things further.

This whole situation is well above my pay grade, and I know better than to get involved in something so politically charged. Zena might be playing with fire, and while I feel for her, I also know how quickly things can go south here.

Chapter 5

The Kidnap

Sunday 19 September 2004

The report below was a shock to us, especially as they were taken from a house just round the corner from us.

Our American clients are so on edge now, I mean, they want us to go with them when going for a piss, I can't blame them considering . . .

Iraq has ruled out concessions to kidnappers threatening to murder British hostage Kenneth Bigley and two American colleagues within hours.

Prime Minister Iyad Allawi said after No 10 talks with Tony Blair that his government was 'trying our best' to free 62-year-old Mr Bigley.

But the country's foreign minister Hoshyar Zebari, also in London, said giving in to the captors' demands to free women prisoners in jails in Abu Ghraib and Um Qasr would set 'a very bad precedent'.

He added: 'Our policy is not to negotiate with the terrorists. These people have an agenda trying to undermine this government, to influence the US elections, even beyond Iraq. They have ideological, very extreme views.'

On Saturday morning the group said it would give the coalition 48 hours to release the women prisoners, or all three hostages would be killed.

Mr Blair confirmed he had discussed the fate of Mr Bigley with Mr Allawi when they met at Downing Street. But both leaders remained tight-lipped about what could be done to secure his release

A video of Mr Bigley and his fellow hostages, blindfolded and with their hands apparently bound, was shown yesterday on Arab TV station Aljazeera.

Footage showed Mr Bigley, Jack Hensley and Eugene Armstrong seated on the floor with their heads bowed, while a masked man stood behind them reading from a sheet of paper. The hostages were seized by terrorists on Thursday during a dawn raid in the wealthy al-Mansour district of the Iraqi capital. They were employed by Gulf Supplies and Commercial Services, a United Arab Emirates, based general services and construction contractor.

Mr Bigley, a twice married father, of, one, originally from the Liverpool area, was said to have ignored both threats and advice to leave the country. His mother Elizabeth, 86, told *The Sunday Mirror*: 'We are beside ourselves with worry. I just don't want them to hurt him. He has not done anything to harm anyone.' Mr Bigley, who had been in Baghdad since shortly after the invasion of Iraq last year, reportedly told neighbours in Iraq he was looking forward to retiring to Thailand to be with his Thai wife.

Tuesday 21 September 2004

Things have really gone tits up with the hostage situation. Eugene Armstrong, the American contractor, was beheaded today, and we were all gathered to watch the footage that was released by the bastards in grim silence. Seeing that kind of brutality up close, even though on screen, makes it impossible to escape the reality of what we're dealing with here. It's not just a war of bullets and bombs anymore; it's psychological. The sheer barbarism of what we witnessed, someone's life snuffed out in such a grotesque, inhumane way, it's left us all rattled to the core.

The room was tense, everyone reacting in their own way, but the sick feeling in our stomachs was shared by all. You hear about these things happening, but when you see it, it's different. It makes the threat more real, more immediate. This isn't something happening to someone far away, it's happening right here, right now, in a house just around the corner from us. These bastards could easily come for us next.

We've talked it over, and there's no debate: if any of us are caught, we've made the pact that we won't let them take us alive. There's no glory in surviving that kind of capture. The thought of being paraded around on camera, used as a pawn for some twisted cause, no one here is willing to face that. I've thought about it over and over, and the thing that keeps coming back to me is the image of my family. I couldn't bear the idea of them watching me in one of those horrific videos, helpless while these fucking cowards butcher me like livestock. The idea of their grief, the helplessness they would feel, it eats away at me.

I've taken my own precautions, like the others. I've got a spare magazine loaded with special rounds, dumdums. These hollow-tipped bullets are nasty, they tear right through flesh, making an absolute mess. They're illegal in most places for a reason, but here, it feels like there are no rules left. I keep that mag close by, and one of those rounds, well, it's got my name on it. I also have a grenade that I strap to my rig, right next to my heart, I will pull that pin! It's not something I ever want to use, but if the worst comes, it's my final insurance policy.

There's a quiet understanding among us now. We all know what's at stake, but no one says it outright. This isn't the kind of thing you joke about or even talk about much.

Saturday 9 October 2004

It's been a while since I last made an entry, life has been chaotic, to say the least. The last few weeks have been a blur, and I'm feeling the weight of it all. The stress has been mounting, and sleep has become a distant memory. My body and mind feel heavy; I'm smoking way more than normal which is killing my lungs and throat. I'm running on fumes, and it's clear I need a break before something gives. But in this environment, there's just no space for downtime. We still have to take our clients out and it's becoming more hostile here than ever.

The news today was gut-wrenching. Kenneth Bigley, the British hostage, was beheaded yesterday by these cowardly terrorists. The footage of his brutal execution is haunting, and my heart aches for his family. What they must be going through is unimaginable knowing that their loved one was subjected to such cruelty. It's a stark reminder of the constant danger we face and how precarious life has become here. I can't stop thinking about the fear he must have felt, the helplessness. It makes you question everything.

In the middle of all this, my phone buzzed. It was a good pal of mine, Billy Mcfatter. We previously worked closely about six years back on a job in the UK. We hadn't spoken in a while. He tells me he's out here now, along with Ian Harris, another familiar face from the old crew. Funny how paths cross again, it's a small world.

I haven't seen them both for years. He's in the Green Zone, working with another company, we can see the Green Zone gates from our house they're not far, but you have to drive around about 5 mins to get to them. It was a chance to catch up, have a beer, and maybe forget about the madness for a little while. The problem was that we didn't have an armoured vehicle available, which is the standard protocol when moving around Baghdad. Normally, we'd need a minimum of two people and a properly kitted-out vehicle for any trip, but that wasn't an option tonight.

Rob, a new bloke who had just arrived in, country, decided he wanted to go too, and we decided to take the only thing we had: a clapped, out minibus, the jingle bus we called it. In hindsight, this was a colossal mistake. But at the time, it seemed like the quickest way to get to see my old muckers. We decided to go in local rag, blend in but driving in Baghdad at night is a whole different beast. The US Military constantly shut down roads, setting up new barriers to isolate insurgents, and it's a nightmare to navigate. What was a clear route one day could be completely blocked off the next. And tonight, as luck would have it, the roads we needed were shut tight. We didn't have a map or any form of GPS, so we were on our own!

It was pitch black, the usual landmarks disappear, and even the smallest wrong turn can lead you into a world of trouble. And that's exactly what happened, we got lost. Not just a little lost either; we ended up over the river, in the heart of Sadr City, a no-go zone if there ever was one. It's where Al-Qaeda and all the militias are based. Think Dodge City on steroids. The moment we realised where we were, the panic started to set in. I felt that cold rush of adrenaline drain from my body, and the feeling of your stomach dropping, leaving behind nothing but a raw sense of isolation and helplessness.

I called one of the lads back at the house, who should have known the way out, but the idiot gave me the wrong directions, making the situation even worse. At this point, I was convinced we weren't getting out alive. I did the only thing I could think of, I called Sarah. I knew there was a real chance that this could be the last time I'd speak to her. I called Sarah, 'Honey, I'm in the shit . . . If I don't make it out, tell Kyle I'm sorry, and I love him.'

I could hear the panic in her voice as she asked what was going on, trying to stay calm. I told her the truth, that we were lost in Baghdad, and there was a chance we wouldn't make it out alive. Sarah's a strong woman, she likes to play the tough card, but I know she worries more than she lets on. I've been on the phone with her before when bombs were going off nearby, and while any normal person would be freaking out, Sarah just asks, 'How close was it?' and keeps the conversation going as if nothing's happening. Once, while I was describing how mortars had taken out a few blokes not far away, she started talking about redecorating the bathroom. It's her way of coping, I think, but underneath it all, I think she's scared more than she lets on.

As we were driving around in circles, Rob and I had one clear thought between us, we were not going to end up on CNN in orange boiler suits. Rob, being American, joked that he'd be first in line to die, which wasn't much comfort. We both had our pistols ready, stashed under our legs as we drove through the dark streets, knowing that if it came to it, we had a pact: we wouldn't let ourselves be captured. The idea of being paraded on TV and having our heads cut off was too much to bear. We agreed, shook hands, and braced ourselves for the worst.

Every junction we came to felt like a death trap. At one point, locals began to surround our van, their faces illuminated in the dim streetlights trying to look into the van, some on their phones looking at us too. My heart was pounding, every instinct screaming at me to flee. This wouldn't be a fight we'd win; the tension was so thick you could almost feel it pressing down on you. At this point, I called my pal Billy who was in the Green Zone, and thank God, he was able to guide us out of the mess we were in. We tore down the wrong side of a highway, lights flashing, shouting 'GET OUT THE FUCKING WAY', not caring about the chaos we were leaving behind. We were like two madmen on a mission to stay alive.

Eventually, we made it to the Green Zone checkpoint. I don't think I've ever been so relieved to see an American soldier in my life. When we got through, we practically fell out of the van. The first thing we did was order two bottles of Bud and downed them in about 10 seconds flat. I called Sarah back to let her know we were safe, and all she said was, 'You fanny!' with that mix of relief and sarcasm only she can pull off. We laughed, but the truth is, it was another one of my lives ticked off.

Chapter 6

Covert Ops

Tuesday 12 October 2004

I've recently stepped into a new role within the company, and this time, it's covert Team leader. I have a new team to work with, and we've been tasked by the Americans with reconnaissance missions on various substations across north-west Iraq. The job involves visiting specific locations from grid references, assessing the hostility, running rout reports, gauging local sentiment, identifying safe areas, hospitals etc and taking pictures to report back. It's a big responsibility, and the paperwork is intense, something I'm not exactly great at, to be honest. Still, it's a privilege to be entrusted with such a specialised task. At the same time, there's always that little voice in my head hoping I don't fuck it up.

Our first mission took us to Al Baghdadi, a town north-west of Baghdad around 250km near the Syrian border. One huge advantage of having an Iraqi team is that they know the roads, understand the mood of the people, and can spot trouble areas in ways we simply can't. I'm sitting in the back seat of our lead vehicle, dressed as a local woman in a burka, well, half a burka as it's cut from the waist down. It's a strange feeling, being armed to the teeth but completely hidden. My driver is a bit of a shady character with connections that you don't ask too much about, but in this job, trust isn't always a luxury, it's a necessity.

Ali, our interpreter, is young and cocky, but he's smart and well, educated. He's the natural leader of the Iraqi side of the team, which helps keep things smooth. My second-in-command, Lee, is in the second vehicle, with his own driver and local guard. Leo's team brings up the rear in the third car. All of our vehicles are fitted with emergency transponders so HQ can track us at all times. In the back of my seat, I've got my AK and pistol, grenades, bags of ammo, cameras, voice recorders, maps, and more water than we'll probably need. Plus, more grenades, because why not?

The hardest part of working like this is keeping a low profile. If the Americans see us, they'll assume we're insurgents. If the locals see us, they'll think we're Mossad agents. It's a no-win situation. We have to move through the streets without drawing attention, which is easier said than done. Every time we hit traffic, it feels like walking a tightrope. Too much attention in either direction could mean trouble.

I can't even count how many times the Americans have mistakenly fired warning shots at us. It's beyond frustrating, feeling like you're dodging threats from both sides. If the Iraqis don't get us, there's a good chance the Americans might.

Chapter 7

The Bomb

As we were driving back from a recce mission in Fallujah, my 2ic radioed me from the second car and asked if I wanted to stop by the Green Zone café for lunch. The café is considered relatively safe, located within the Green Zone and run by locals, but the scoff is decent. For some reason, though, I had a gut feeling that made me say no. I told him, 'Let's just head back to base.' I couldn't explain it at the time, but something didn't feel right.

Not long after, one of the lads from our HQ called me and said there had been an explosion at the café, and a few of our guys were there. Immediately, I got on the phone to the OC, and then it was a mad scramble to get information. We didn't know much at first, just that Mick, Rob, and Stuart from another of our teams were all in bad shape. Turns out, while they were having lunch, some bastard walked in with a briefcase full of explosives and blew the place to fuck.

Me and a couple of lads went straight to the military hospital to see them, and the sight of them was a real shock. Mick told us how he was blown clear across the room. When he came to, he realised he was on fire. His head was split open, and blood was pouring out as he tried to roll around and put out the flames. He lost his clothes in the blast, they were just gone, blown off his body. Somehow, despite everything, Mick managed to scramble out of the café, bleeding and burned, but instead of collapsing, he went back in to rescue an unconscious man lying inside. Naked and burnt, he dragged the man out, then walked 200 yards to the American Combat Support Hospital. I don't know where he found the strength. Shock and sheer determination must have kicked in.

Mick's lost most of his ear, his face is a mess, and his whole body is riddled with shrapnel wounds. He's a hard man but seeing him like that, it's tough.

Stuart, though, is in even worse shape. When we passed his hospital room, he saw us and mumbled, 'Scott . . . lads . . .' As soon as we walked in, he started crying, begging us, 'Please take me home, I want to go home.' It hit me hard, seeing him like that. This was a man who had always been a strong bloke reduced to a fragile wreck. I felt a lump in my throat and my eyes began to sting as I tried to hold back tears. It's surreal, watching your buddy crumble in front of you.

Stu was trying to eat a banana while sobbing, and the whole thing just felt bizarre. He was probably on a lot of pain meds too. I did my best to comfort him, telling him he was going to be okay, trying to lighten the mood by saying, 'You're going home, you lucky fucker, and on full pay too!' But he wasn't hearing any of it. He just kept mumbling, 'Scotty, take me home, please, get me out of here.' I leaned over and grabbed his hand. This wasn't a time for bravado or being tough; it was a time for compassion. Stu had lost an eye, some teeth, and had a hole in his head about the size of a ping pong ball. His leg and back were badly burned, and his entire body was peppered with shrapnel. He told us through painful mumbles he saw the bomber walk in and detonate right next to their table. The next thing he knew, bits of bodies were all over him as he staggered out of the café, still on fire, before collapsing.

Rob's condition is even worse. He was completely unconscious when we got the news, with half his face blown away. He's lost his lip, cheekbone, and part of his ear, and most of his body is burned. We didn't get to see him in the hospital because they flew him directly to a military hospital in Tikrit. Rob and I became especially close after that night we got lost in Baghdad, and knowing he's in such a critical state is shit. Seeing your mates like this, strong men, reduced to these broken, fragile states shakes you up, especially when you think, shit If we went there, that would have been us!

My good pal Bob approached me this morning with an offer that I wasn't expecting. He mentioned an investor he'd been talking to, someone willing to pay good money for us to set up our own company in Kuwait. The investor's idea was to run convoys from Kuwait to Baghdad, one of the most dangerous routes at the time, but we'd have full control. We could pick our own teams, make our own decisions, and essentially call the shots.

I wasn't really looking to jump ship, but the money was almost double what I was making now, although, with that came double the danger. Still, I couldn't help but think about it. If I did this for a few months, I could get out of the sandpit altogether, head back to Scotland, and maybe even set up my own operation there. After all, I'd been in, country for three years, and I was starting to feel like I was burning through my nine lives at an alarming rate.

After mulling it over, I agreed to meet the investor and hear him out. We laid out what we needed, vehicles, weapons, the right equipment, and a solid crew. We didn't hold back, listing our fee, the gear we required, and even the accommodation we expected. To my surprise, the investor seemed keen and hung on every word. He was already a wealthy man, but this venture could make him millions.

When I go on leave, I will take an extended break and have a go at this new outfit.

Chapter 8

Tactical Defence Ltd.

Friday 18 March 2005

So, I get a call from Bob. 'It's on', he said . . . the investor will agree to everything so, we're heading out there to get things sorted, will meet you there next week.'

A few weeks passed, and true to his word, the equipment began arriving daily. Brand new Toyota Land Cruisers, all modified to our exact specifications, extra-large fuel tanks for long journeys, good comms etc. We were even set up in a decent hotel in Kuwait City, a far cry from the rough accommodations I'd gotten used to. Bob, being ex-Regiment, knew the kind of men we needed and pulled in a few more blokes to round out the crew.

It all felt surreal, the idea of running my own show, choosing my team, and making the big decisions. But as much as the opportunity was enticing, the risks were just as real. The convoys up to Baghdad were like running the gauntlet, and we all knew it. Still, the thought of being able to finally get out of this place and go back home was tempting enough to keep me moving forward.

As the new outfit started to take shape, we managed to bring on board some of the locals we had worked with back in Basra. These guys weren't just random hires; we had a history with them. They had fought alongside us in the past, and there was a level of trust there that you just can't buy. Of course, we offered them good money to sweeten the deal, but the real currency was the bond we'd built through shared combat. They knew the lay of the land, and we knew they had our backs when it counted.

The first couple of convoys went relatively smoothly. The equipment and vehicles we had were top quality, but there was always a catch, those Toyota Land Cruisers we were using were soft skins, not armoured. They weren't fully kitted out like the heavy, duty 4x4s we'd sometimes rolled in. If we took a serious hit or ambushed, there was no guarantees. Rounds could come through like a hot knife through butter. It was another gamble in a long line of risks we were taking for the money.

We were tasked with taking a convoy to Al Rashid power station at 0600hrs, just as the first light of dawn was starting to creep over the horizon. Visibility was still low, and the dim morning haze made it difficult to see far ahead. As we navigated through the traffic, we passed an Iraqi Police checkpoint. We stopped at the main gates of the power plant, big smooth iron ones around 12ft high. We held the traffic around 100m away from us as we have to do this after the number of cars that would come close to your convoy and detonate, taking you all out. I heard the unmistakable crack of a gunshot fired into the air. A few moments later, a white minibus, about 100m in front of us with the civilian traffic behind them suddenly screeched to a halt, reversed, and a group of insurgents jumped out, armed to the teeth with automatic weapons.

At that point, we were sitting ducks, stopped right in front of the main gate to the power station, waiting for entry. But no one was opening the fucking gates for us! The locals, who were standing outside waiting to get into their work panicked and started trying to climb the tall smooth steel gates with their fingernails, eyes open wide with fear, like scared rats. It was obvious the Iraqi police were in on it, the signal shot they fired must have initiated the ambush. The noise was deafening as the insurgents opened up with their weapons. Our own Iraqi guards, to their credit, started firing back from their Gun truck we had kitted out with a GPMG, but I could see they were mostly shooting into the air, over the traffic, laying down suppressive fire rather than aiming at anything specific.

The incoming rounds were whizzing past my face as I was trying to find cover. I dived behind a concrete wall. I could see the insurgents were using the local cars as cover. I couldn't get a clean shot without risking hitting civilians, families, kids, anyone who was unlucky enough to be in the wrong place at the wrong time. That hesitation weighed on me, knowing I had to act, but not recklessly.

I threw myself back into the fight, adrenaline kicking into high gear. Just as I got back into position, a round clipped my body armour. For a split second, I thought fuck! My heart stopped, but the rush of adrenaline took over, numbing the fear. I had no time to dwell on it, I had a responsibility to my team, and I needed to get them into cover. We couldn't hold out in the open much longer.

After what felt like an eternity, but in reality, was probably only 1 or 2 minutes, the gate finally creaked open. Bullets were still flying in both directions as I shouted to everyone to move, get inside the camp, now! Somehow, through the chaos, we all managed to get inside the compound, diving for cover as the gates closed behind us.

Once inside, I did a quick headcount, making sure everyone was accounted for. Remarkably, we had all made it through unscathed. As we checked each other over, the sheer disbelief set in, how the hell had we survived that? There must have been dozens of rounds flying past us, and yet no one was injured. I could feel my pulse starting to come down, but the realisation hit hard, not again!

This job is not what I imagined it would be. I've been pushing hard for funding to up-armour the vehicles, but we're still stuck running around in soft skins. Our investor keeps telling me he's 'working on it', but honestly, I'm not holding my breath. The reality is, I'm at the point now where I'm pissed off every time we head out on a mission. We're exposed, completely vulnerable, we are just one ambush away from disaster.

What makes it worse is that we're only one small team, with no backup, no Quick Reaction Force (QRF), and no military assistance. We're on our own out here, isolated in a massive war zone with no one to call if things go south. The more I think about it, the more it pisses me off. If a well-armed militia cell decided to step out in front of our convoy, we'd be sitting ducks. One good burst from an automatic weapon and those bullets would slice through the soft skin vehicles with ease.

The shitty part? No one would ever know. We could disappear off the face of the earth without a trace. No one would come looking for us, not the military, not the local authorities. One ambush, one attack, and we'd vanish into the chaos. It's hard to put into words the weight of that realisation, knowing that out here, in the middle of this war zone, we're utterly on our own. Most decent outfits would have a QRF and other teams ready to deploy scattered around the country, this is not what I asked for.

OK, Picture this . . . 2100hrs pitch black, no lights for miles, one road – a dual carriageway which slices through the deserted roads at this time the most dangerous area in the world!

Yep you got it, yours truly stuck between Baghdad and Fallujah on the Main Road at nighttime with 4 high profile soft skin Land Cruisers. This is worst case scenario, all because I was teamed up with 2 alcoholic Brit rejects who wanted to head into Baghdad for a fucking drink!

We were taking concrete t-walls to camp Fallujah from Kuwait which is about a 12-hour drive. We arrived in Fallujah about 1600hrs and were told we could sleep in the camp overnight before heading back to Kuwait. All is good until the Military realise that we have an Iraqi team with us and decide that we couldn't bring them into camp. Us three Brits were ok but not these guys, so I suggested as TL that we just stay in the bases car park area which was safe. We could sleep in the vehicles for one night, no big dramas until one of my internationals decided to start a fuckin coup. He was looking to go into Baghdad and stay in a hotel so he could have a beer and a nice comfy bed! This wasn't just a quick 5-minute detour, this was at least an hour's drive in the dark of night. This guy had no idea about security; he was ex-SAS but an alcoholic with just one thing on his mind.

He managed to get all the local Iraqis on board with his idea and the other Brit lad that was in our team.

'Are you fuckin serious?' I said, 'You are willing to risk your lives for a comfy bed and a beer!' I couldn't believe it.

I had no choice, they had rebelled against me so I thought fuck it, Let's go and get shot to fuck and when the locals have us captured in orange boiler suits, I can turn to these fucks and say, told you so dickheads

I took lead and thought if we make it, I am out from this clown outfit. We must have got about 3 miles down this black lonely road when I saw the rear lights of vehicles ahead. As we approached there was about 4 local Iraqi cars all stopped, they could not move forward as there was an American patrol up ahead. I decided to get out and try and walk to the yanks with my hands up and flashcards showing, we call it the Walk of chance, the chance someone in the local cars takes a pop, the chance the patrol doesn't like the look of us and shoots. All about chance. I was hoping they had night vision!! We certainly couldn't hang about here much longer.

As I made my way through the local vehicles to the front the Iraqis were looking at me as if I was fucking crazy, I saw one or two on mobile phones and thought they might be calling their friendly militia buddies.

I must have got 10ft in front of the waiting locals when a tracer round was fired at me, obviously a warning shot. Fuck, these guys think I am a local, best not to go any further.

As I was walking back to my vehicle, I heard Adnan my local driver shouting on the radio . . . 'Mr Scott, militia coming, quick!'

What he was trying to tell me was that a militia cell had been informed that a lost easy target was stuck outside Fallujah. I quickly ran back to my car and as I did, I could see the pick-ups coming from both directions over the desert, Adnan my driver is in bits and telling me we are going to die. A strange feeling . . . when you are in an ambush or contact, your training takes over and your brain goes into auto pilot with no fear, just adrenaline. When you are abandoned on a dark road with no help and the prospect of dying a slow painful death that's the shit part of this job.

At this point I shout over the comms to switch off all lights, turn around and drive back to camp Fallujah, nice and slowly we sneak away until we are out of sight then whack the lights on and drive the cars like we stole them! We pitch up at Camp Fallujah which is in complete darkness and lockdown so we can't get in.

I was so angry at this point, I called Bob, back in Kuwait and told him to get me a flight out ASAP. I couldn't work with these piss head idiots anymore. I have never been so close to killing someone in cold blood before, but I could have easily slotted these two bellends that night.

I decided to keep calm as I had to drive back with them in the morning, so told them to stag on each an hour and keep watch while we slept just outside the gate.

ON LEAVE AGAIN. I'm back home now, I took a few weeks off to try and recover from the absolute chaos of that last tour. I wish I could say it's been easy, but if I'm honest, my head's a bit all over the place. My mental state is fried, no doubt about it. I can't even drive through my own town without feeling like I'm back out there. Every trip down the road feels like a mission, and I'm scanning for threats, Plastic bags, potholes, random debris, I'm dodging them like they're about to blow me to bits. I catch myself swerving, my heart racing, then I must pull it together. 'Snap out of it, Scott!' I tell myself. But it's like my body is stuck in survival mode and won't let go.

Two days ago, I was dodging bullets, trying to stay alive in a place where death was an everyday companion. Now I'm standing in Tesco's, pushing a cart around like nothing happened, trying to decide what to have for dinner. I mean, which world is real? And which is fake? The shift between those two extremes is mind-bending, and honestly, I'm struggling to figure out where I fit in.

I want to adjust back, I really do, but Jesus, it's not as simple as coming home and flicking a switch. The other night, I was having dinner with my wife and some friends. They were talking about their jobs and all the stress they're under. One of my friend's husband across from me was going on about some big project at the bank, how tough it is managing deadlines, office politics, and the rest of it. And I'm sitting there, biting my tongue, thinking, 'Mate, are you fucking serious? Try dodging RPGs, watching the horrors of War. That's stress. That's pressure.' I couldn't help but feel like I was from another planet, listening to people whose reality just doesn't make sense to me anymore. They're good people, but these are not my people. This is not my world. I don't belong here.

I feel it in my bones: this version of life, with its office jobs and everyday stresses, isn't where I'm meant to be right now. I can't stop thinking about going back, where things make sense, even if it's dangerous as hell. Out there, at least I know the rules. Get me back to the sandpit, because here… here, I'm just lost.

Chapter 9

I've Missed You Guys

Thursday 12 May 2005, I'M BACK WITH THE LADS

I'm back with my original outfit. I spoke to the PM and asked if he would take me back, his reply surprised me saying of course Scotty, we need good men like you, call the office and I'll sort it out. Rob is the gaffer out here, a superb guy, he's ex-Regiment too like most of them. I have the utmost respect for the older blokes who have been doing this most of their lives.

There are loads of new characters here, I am sharing a room with one of the funniest guys I have met. Big Vinny is about 6ft 2, 17 stone, tattoos etc. Looks mean as fuck but is the softest pussycat, a proper laugh. although I reckon that would turn if you pissed him off.

Vinny loves to shock the lads, walking around the house completely bollock naked. Of course, everyone shouts at him to put some fucking clothes on, and he always fires back in his best camp voice, 'Oh, am I turning you on, boys? Bet you wish you had a cock like mine!' Then, the big idiot tucks his knob between his legs and prances around like he's some sort of woman. A bit of craic like that goes a long way in a place like this.

There are about fifteen of us living in this one house, most of whom I've known since the beginning. Take Yves Morange, for example, he and I started around the same time back in 2003. He's a French, speaking Croat, no stranger to war, and I've always admired him for his cool, calm demeanour. Nothing seems to rattle the guy.

I've always been one of the first up in the morning, mainly because I like to head out on a full stomach. But the catch was, if you were up early, you had to make everyone's coffee. Yves, though, was always a bit of a nightmare about it. He'd give me his best French accent and say, 'It's all about the consistency, Scotty!' He had this thing where the colour and the level of the coffee had to be absolutely perfect, or he wouldn't touch it. That right there sums up Yves, everything had to be just right. You could see it in how he approached everything, not just his coffee.

Another one of our teams was hit whilst coming back to Baghdad on a mission yesterday. Saito, Nick, and sixteen local nationals got lost and landed up in real shit territory. For what we can gather, they were seen checking the map when the militia started setting up a highly complex ambush.

All we know is that the ambush was initiated with an IED and when the guys were out fighting, they took cover but were overwhelmed. Nick managed to escape to tell us everyone else was slaughtered by these bastards. To our disbelief the militia had filmed it and put it on a website. They have claimed to have captured Saito, as his ID cards were all over the net. And on the news back home.

When we spoke to Nick who was the only survivor of the attack, he said they were running for cover towards a garage as they were out of ammo, when Saito was hit in the back of the head. Nick said he went down straight away, totally gone in just a second. Poor guy didn't know what hit him, probably the best thing as we could not bear the thought of him being captured and beheaded by this scum. Another top bloke gone in a blink of an eye.

Below is a report from a newspaper.

May 8, 2005
Japanese Hostage, Akihiko Saito, Died After Shooting According to Terrorist Video Islamic militant group Army

of Ansar al-Sunna said it has killed a Japanese hostage and posted footage allegedly showing his bloodied body, according to an Internet video.

The video showed identification papers and a passport bearing the name of Akihiko Saito, 44, a former paratrooper and veteran of the French Foreign Legion, who had been missing in Iraq since May 8.

The footage, which was not dated but was seen by Reuters on Saturday, showed the body of a dead man lying on his back with blood covering his face. He appeared to resemble Saito's pictures.

'This is your punishment . . . infidel' shouted an unseen man to the background of gunshots.

The Japanese Foreign Ministry said it was trying to confirm if the body was Saito's, a ministry spokesman said.

'We have not confirmed that,' said Akira Chiba, assistant press secretary for the foreign ministry, adding that confirmation was difficult from simply watching the footage.

Earlier this month, Army of Ansar al, Sunna said it had seriously injured Saito after they abducted him in an ambush of a convoy of cars coming from a US base near Baghdad.

A statement accompanying the video said the group shot and killed Saito.

ID papers said Saito worked as a security manager.

Army of Ansar al-Sunna, one of the main Sunni Muslim insurgent groups, has claimed responsibility for attacks against US forces and the Iraqi government and killed several hostages.

May 15, 2005

New Video by Ansar al-Sunnah Army Shows Japanese Ambush in Iraq

A militant group that allegedly kidnapped a Japanese man in Iraq has released a new video apparently showing the scene of the ambush that led to his capture, a Japanese news agency reports.

The Ansar al-Sunnah Army claimed on its website last week that it ambushed a group of five foreign workers, killing four and kidnapping the fifth, Japanese citizen Akihito Saito, 44.

Tokyo has been unable to independently confirm Saito's whereabouts or condition.

The group's website had a new video purportedly showing their attack, but Saito's image could not be confirmed, Japan's Kyodo News agency reported from Cairo.

Japan's Foreign Ministry said it couldn't immediately confirm the report.

An unidentified man who survived the ambush has told Japanese officials that Saito was severely bleeding after being shot and it was unlikely that he could have survived.

Japanese Foreign Minister Nobutaka Machimura said the government had tried to contact the captors through intermediaries: 'We are trying everything we can, but so far he has not been found.'

Last year, when five Japanese were taken hostage in Iraq and later released, many Japanese criticised them for recklessly endangering themselves.

In October, when Iraqi militants beheaded a Japanese backpacker, many in Japan blamed the victim for his own death.

But those incidents also fuelled opposition to Japan's presence in Iraq. Many Japanese have criticised it as a violation of Japan's pacifist constitution.

As you can imagine the morale of the camp is low as there were good men killed here.

7 June 2005

Another ambush. Twenty-eight days since the last one, but this one hit harder, much harder.

Yves, Paddy, Denis, and Sean were tasked with protecting a convoy of beds, yeah, *beds*, to an American military camp near Najaf. I mean, fucking *beds*!

The night before, I had a bad feeling. I told Yves, *I knew* something was wrong. The intel wasn't good, and even the locals were saying it was a mistake. I begged him to reconsider, to talk to the Boss to get the mission reassessed. I pleaded with him. I told him straight, I'd had a dream he was going to die. My gut was screaming at me that this was wrong. But Yves, in his usual way, just brushed me off: 'I am being paid to do a job. If I die, I die, Scotty.' He even walked up and down the room playing the death march on his laptop, laughing and mocking fate perhaps?

Yves was one of the calmest, strongest of the men in our squad, strong in mind and spirit, as well as body. If you can picture him, he was 5ft 10in, fit, muscular, always wearing a cheeky grin and always had a funny comeback. He had his share of scars and was even missing a finger, but it never slowed him down.

He had this cavalier attitude, like nothing could touch him. He'd talk about death like it was no big deal, like he had already made his peace with it. His military training kept him sharp, and his Iraqi team members respected the hell out of him. They'd follow him into the fire without a second thought. They were that strong a unit.

Then there was Denis, cut from the same cloth. A highly decorated Sergeant Major from the French Foreign Legion. A man of few words but the kind who commanded respect just by being in the room. His experience was unparalleled, and his piercing eyes spoke volumes. Then there was Paddy, another Legionnaire from Ireland, quick with a joke, always lifting the mood no matter how dark things got.

The team was en route, moving steadily through a series of US checkpoints. At each stop, the Americans warned them, 'Turn back. Don't go there, the last two convoys to come through were attacked with no survivors.' Every team that had taken this route before them had been hit. But Yves was laser focused on the mission. He never questioned orders, no matter how grim the warnings. So, they pressed on, determined to get the job done.

They reached Al Habania, travelling along a high berm road when everything went sideways. One of the escort vehicles, commanded by Dennis, got stuck and was immobilized, making them vulnerable. Paddy, scanning the area, spotted a man 100m away, in a house, taking up position with a rifle. Without hesitating, Paddy fired into the area and shouted, 'Contact left, Contact left!'

Immediately, they were hit by a force of over thirty men, covering every exit, cutting off any chance of escape.

Sean and his team pushed their vehicle forward passing Denis into the kill zone, trying to offer help. Meanwhile, Denis, stuck at the rear, vehicle immobilised, was fighting his own battle, doing what he could, killing at short range till he was almost out of bullets. In the midst of all this chaos, Yves was on the radio, calling back to Rob, the Boss, in HQ. 'Contact, Contact, men down, send backup . . . send backup.' I was in the office when the call came through. I could hear the gunfire and the Iraqis shouting and screaming. I jumped up, shouted down to my team to get ready for a QRF (Quick reaction force), getting the cars and weapons prepped at double speed. I told the boss we were going in to help.

He told us to prepare but wait till he gave the order; he wanted the full picture first expecting the US military to get there. I was pacing, furious, pleading with him to let us go. 'Let us fucking' go, boss, come on!! 'I shouted. But he kept saying, 'Wait.' And then the comms with Yves went dead.

The silence was torture. We waited to hear from the US military, and when the news finally came through . . . it was bad.

It took 36 hours before Denis and Paddy made it back to camp. They were wrecked, dirty, bloody, and in shock. We didn't say a word as they walked through the gates, looking like they couldn't even process what had happened. I met Denis's eyes, and they were hollow, emotionless. I held out my hand and grabbed him, but no words were exchanged, just a hard embrace. The weight of everything they'd lost hung heavy in the air.

They went to see the boss for a debrief while we sat in silence, numb, thinking of our lost brothers.

Paddy was the first to come in and tell us what had happened.

He said during the firefight, he used his car as a shield, returning fire, but accidentally shot a round into Yves's car. Yves, in the middle of calling for assistance, still managed to shout, 'Oi, you crazy fucker, watch my car!' That was Yves, always cracking jokes, even in the worst situations.

Sean, trying to provide support, drove his car straight into the kill zone. He passed Denis's disabled vehicle a move that likely saved Denis's life. But the second Sean stepped out of his car, he was shot and killed instantly. Yves kept shouting to his Iraqi team, 'The Yanks are coming, hold it together!' But when he locked eyes with Paddy, there was something helpless in his expression. It was as if he knew, they were on their own.

The Iraqi team were dropping one by one, screaming and crying, trying to fight back under impossible odds. Yves and Paddy were running out of ammo. Then, Paddy saw it, Yves took a shot to the stomach. He collapsed, falling to his knee, locking eyes with Paddy one last time before he died.

Paddy had no bullets left, no choice but to run. He crawled over the bodies of their fallen men and made a dash for one of the cars. As he was running, he was shot in the leg and face but still managed to get up, searching for a weapon, but there was nothing left. He rolled down a berm into a ditch, threw off his body armour, and climbed into a sewage pipe, full of shit and piss. He lay there for 45 minutes, with only inches of air to breathe, listening to the enemy above, blowing up what was left and firing into the bodies of the already dead.

He heard them talking about Yves, saying he looked like the leader, and then they dragged his body in front of a car and ran over him, repeatedly.

Dennis, meanwhile, managed to hijack a local vehicle and tried to rejoin the fight, but the trucks were in flames, and there was no way through. He had no choice but to get out of there and find an American checkpoint to get help.

A USAF A-10 screeched by, dropping a 500lb bomb on the place. Paddy, still in the pipe, was praying they wouldn't get him too. He said he wasn't a very religious man, but on this occasion, he pleaded with God to hear him.

It turned out The Americans had decided not to engage in a land fight to help the team as there was no US personnel involved; their SOP was just to flatten the area.

When the bombs and shooting finally stopped, Paddy crawled out of the pipe. As he emerged, he saw the barrel of an Abrams tank pointed right at him. Barely standing, covered in blood, he stumbled toward the tank. The Americans patched him up and got him to a hospital.

As we sat there, listening to Paddy tell us what happened, the room was silent. Devastation doesn't even cover it. We couldn't speak, each of us trapped in our own thoughts, picturing the hell they'd gone through. Yves was more than a brilliant operator, he was a brother and a fierce warrior. We'll never forget him.

The next day, the Rob, the boss, decided we should have a beer to honour Yves, Sean and the lads. After dinner, we headed up to the roof of our compound. We sat, talking shit, laughing at memories of Yves and his funny ways. made a toast, and we all reflected on life, on family, on this fucked up place. It was a strange, sombre, yet peaceful night. One of those moments where everything just slows down, and the reality of it all hits you like a freight train.

After six relentless months on deployment, I figured it was time to take a break, to try and settle back into civilian life. I went home, hoping to reconnect with the world I'd left behind. But no matter how hard I tried; I just didn't fit in anymore. Three years in the war zone had changed me in ways I couldn't shake. Everything that used to feel normal now felt foreign. The bond with the lads, the rush of the job, that had become my reality. Nothing here came close. I couldn't snap out of the hypervigilance. Every car backfiring made me jump, I drove like I was still in a convoy, and the road rage, I didn't even recognize myself. I didn't want to admit it, but I think this was the start of the mental journey with PTSD.

I think it kind of hit when one night I dragged Sarah out of bed by her feet shouting 'contact' and another time I woke up to find her sobbing, when I asked what's wrong she said I sat up, grabbed her throat tight and said, move and I'll fucking kill you!

Maybe I need to go back out there . . . I'll try the normal life for a bit, see how that works out.

I've had enough of this place. I can't stand it anymore, the fake, mundane routine of so, called 'normal' life. This isn't my reality. My real world is out there, where things make sense, where everything has purpose. A friend reached out, said there's a company in

Sean, Yves and Denis

Afghanistan looking for team leaders. Without hesitation, I got the number and made the call. After a short conversation in a pub over a pint, they offered me a position, just like that. Within a week, I was set to deploy. Back to where I belong, however not to the familiarity of Iraq, but to a new adventure in Afghanistan.

Chapter 10

Afghanistan

February 2006

I arrived in Kabul today. Travelled with a good lad, ex-1 Para called Gaz. A little younger than me but he, like myself, had spent the last few years in Iraq and fancied a change too. We have got to know each other well as we've been travelling for 16 hours together.

So, Kabul . . . well, it's an absolute shithole. Been here a few days now, and I never thought I would say this, but it's worse than Iraq. I spent three years in Iraq and thought I'd seen the worst of it... but Kabul? It's on another level.

The place is a rancid, dusty mess. Sewage flows openly in the streets just like Basra but worse, stinking to high heaven, I've nearly puked more than once from the smell. Thanks to the Russians and their landmines migrating down from the mountains every year, the city is full of people missing limbs, men, women, even kids. There's this one guy I see every day on the same corner, no eyes, tattered clothes, one leg, leaning against a post, just trying to survive, begging for whatever he can get. Most of the beggars are high on heroin, as Afghanistan has all the poppy plants, it's so easily available, and cheap.

It feels like these people are stuck in the fourteenth century. No real infrastructure, disease everywhere. It really hits you just how damn lucky we are in the West.

We're here to train and lead two teams of Nepali guards. The head of the group was an old Gurkha Sergeant Major. He kept them in line,

Right: Gerry and I in
the Garden of Eden /
The Adam tree

Below: Garamesh
Camp

With Iraqi team.

Denis, Yves and Sean.

Bob and I at Khor Az zubaiya

Covert Recce missions

Flying into Afghanistan with General Scott and Admiral Dussault

Afghanistan

Receive an award from General Scott.

Saying farewell to the General and welcoming Admiral Dussault.

Left: The day after we caught Saddam in the local newspaper.

Below: Two powerful generals meeting.

Above left: With my thoughts.

Above right: Lead Vehicle hit with IED on route Pluto (Baghdad).

Right: Checkpoint 12, entrance to the Green Zone (Baghdad).

Below: On the road to Baghdad.

The day after the 'Green Zone' cafe suicide bomber.

Kells and I ....
my saviour.

no doubt about it, but he had to be pushing 60. Bow legged and a bit scatty, but still as keen as mustard.

Every morning, right after breakfast, he had them lined up for inspection. If their boots were dirty or their shirts had a crease, he'd go mad. Exactly what I expected from such a proud unit.

Gaz and I have about a month to get these guys up to speed, everything from driving, close protection drills to weapon skills and combat trauma. The pressure's on because we've got clients from the US State Department arriving soon. Their mission? To update and train prison staff at Afghanistan's highest-security facility. That facility is Pul-e-charkhi prison, just a few kilometres east of Kabul. It's home to some of the worst terrorists on the planet, Taliban leaders, Al-Qaeda operatives, and every kind of dangerous extremist you can imagine.

We've been working hard every day, and these blokes take it and never complain, they are a different breed of men. The outfit I'm working with has three houses in Kabul, each equipped with perimeter walls and a 24-hour guard force. These guards, much like in Iraq, are local Afghans provided by someone known as the 'Commander'.

The commander works with us, as long as the money keeps flowing. He ensures our safety, supplies his own men, and lives comfortably here. We all know he's a dangerous guy, a real bastard, but it's far easier, and safer, to have him on our side than against us. It's a bit like the Sheikh we had in Baghdad; you'll be surprised the lengths you go to have an inside man.

The Bosses are mainly South African, a good bunch of guys, again like some of the guys from Iraq, from Selous scouts and South African Military. None of the guys here have done tours in Iraq so they look at Gaz and I with a bit of respect and basically leave us to do our own thing.

I've become good friends with a guy named Bevan, a superb, big man, ex-South African Defence Force. He's got loads of charisma and a calm, professional demeanour. Bevan spent years with special forces in intelligence, and it shows. He's an astute and clever bloke, always a few steps ahead.

George van Schalkwyk is the Country Director. Like Bevan, spent his time with special forces in South Africa. He has a commanding presence, a laid-back guy, tall with jet-black hair, always well, dressed, and never seen without his Beretta pistol and an MP5 slung over his shoulder.

We've also got a contingent of Macedonians working with us, and they all l seem to be related somehow. Kalco is the main man among them; the others look up to him as he struts around like a peacock, acting like he's the dog's bollocks. He and his so called Macedonian mafia work closely with the 'Commander'. Whatever they're up to is anyone's guess, but I stick to what I know best and leave them to it.

Gaz and I were handed a batch of Indian AK-47s to inspect and check, so we took them to the Afghan army range to test them out. We gave a few to our Nepali guards, and it turned into an absolute comedy sketch. Rounds jamming in the chamber, constant stoppages, every time they'd pick one up, it was the same story. 'Fucked!' they'd shout before tossing it aside, only to grab another with identical issues. These were supposed to be the weapons that would save our lives out here. Out of twenty rifles, only two were serviceable.

We loaded up the rest into our vehicles and prepared to head back. As we were getting ready to leave, we noticed the Afghan army training on our left. Suddenly, one of those fuckwit Afghan soldiers had a brain fart and fired an RPG right across our cars. Seriously, what the hell? Is this the 'calibre' of their army?

We found out today that its new year in Nepal. Gaz and I felt honoured when we were asked to be guests at the Nepalese New Year party tonight. They had an amazing spread, filled us with beer, and the Sgt Major delivered a proud speech to the young ones. They have a cake with the year 2063, yes that's right it's officially 2063 in Nepal.

They somehow managed to head into Kabul and buy a goat. After slaughtering it, they served it up in an incredible spread. Once we finished eating, they put on some Nepalese music and treated us to their traditional dance, it was mesmerising and funny at the same time, imagine all these soldiers pissed up doing this weird dancing. Afterward, both Gaz and I were presented with our very own Kukri. They told us, 'Never draw it from its sheath unless it's to spill blood.'

The Pub

After another hard and testing day training the lads Gaz, Bevan and I decided to go to the United Nations bar in Kabul centre. There were a few bars and restaurants here that we could go if we wore local clothes and drove local vehicles, they were relatively safe especially at night.

We had to check our weapons at the door, leaving the rifles in the car and handing over our pistols. As we headed up the stairs, the scene was surprisingly civilized. There were people from all over the world, mostly working for the United Nations. Western music played in the background, and the bar was heavy with cigarette smoke. It felt like a real treat for us.

We were getting slowly pissed when it hit us, 'Shit, better not get too hammered. We still have to drive back.' Gaz was absolutely bursting for a piss, but the line for the toilet was a mile long. 'Cover me for a minute, mate,' he said, clearly up to no good. Next thing I know, he's pissing into a pint glass, filling it right to the brim. He then placed it smack in the middle of the table we were standing at, just as an Afghan couple wandered over.

With the straightest of faces, Gaz picked up the glass, took a mouthful, and pressed his lips together like a wine connoisseur savouring a vintage. 'Something's not right about this wine,' he muttered, holding the glass up for inspection. Then, turning to the Afghan woman, he asked, 'Do you like wine?' She nodded, a bit unsure. Gaz, not missing a beat, extended the glass towards her, 'Here, taste this one, it's got a funny taste!'

Yip, she took a sip of his warm piss, immediately spat it out, gagging in disgust. We were trying so hard not to laugh, but then her boyfriend grabbed the glass and took a swig himself. He wasn't as shy about expressing his opinion, he went fucking ape shit!

He started shouting while we were doubled over in fits of laughter. Then he ran off to get this little bouncer brandishing an AK-47. 'Get out, get out!' the bouncer yelled, and we were promptly escorted from the bar, still in hysterics.

We got outside after collecting our weapons and the bouncer is still shouting at us, Bevan started on him, 'Calm down, you going to fucking shoot us? Go on then fucking asshole' were some of the abuse that was hurled at him while still laughing. Needless to say, we never went back, this was a moment of good banter in this shit hole, it was worth every drop of piss!

During the day, we're busy training the guys, doing recces, and gathering kit or equipment to get ready for the job. But at night? There's fuck all to do but get pissed and get up to some mischief.

Gaz and I share a house with four South African blokes who love a scoop and a braai (BBQ). These guys will throw anything on the grill, from steak to whatever roadkill they can find!

It was my birthday last night, so naturally, a BBQ and a piss-up on the roof of our complex was in order. It all started off civilized until we cracked open the whisky.

'Bet ya my tracer can go further than yours!' Gaz shouts. 'Bollocks, you twat, bet mine will!' Next thing you know, the two of us are firing rounds into the air to see whose tracer would reach further. Bad idea. Then, once all the drink was gone and the South Africans bugged out, Gaz and I thought it'd be a laugh to see how far we could chuck our plastic chairs off the roof. I can't remember much after that. I'm never drinking whisky again!

So, this morning, we're feeling rough as a badger's arse and a bit sheepish. The boss wants to see us. Wonder what that's about, eh?

We took the bollocking and promised we wouldn't do it again. Turns out, the garden where the chairs landed belonged to the Minister of Interior's house. He didn't find it funny.

I don't know what's going on in my head lately. This kind of behaviour isn't me. Is it the chaos of Iraq finally catching up with me, or have I developed some kind of death wish? I feel invincible, taking risks I'd never even consider under normal circumstances.

Kabul has a different feeling from Baghdad; it has a government and laws with police actually having respect here. Back in Baghdad most of the cops were part of the militia and we had a green light to shoot them if they attacked.

Our house has two sections, one for Gaz and I and the South African lads and the other holds the Macedonian mafia.

This consists of four blokes and three women, the men do whatever it is with the 'Commander' and the women do admin. The blokes all look at us with this mean stare and stay away from us which can be awkward as we all have to share the kitchen etc.

I've always been a friendly guy, and I was getting sick of the whole 'them and us' vibe. So, I decided to confront it head, on. I waited until they were all in the living room, sitting down for dinner they'd prepared for themselves. I was starving since I hadn't eaten, so I walked right in, sat down in the middle of them, smiled, and asked how they were, how was their day?

Kalco, the head of the so, called 'Mafia', glared at me and, in a show of masculinity, placed his pistol on the table slowly, like the original gangster, I just chuckled to myself.

After about 10 minutes, though, they softened up, offering me food and chatting about football. Turns out, they were quite friendly, and the women ended up cooking us a fantastic meal!

Our main task here is to transport US State Department officials to Pul-e-Charkhi prison, just outside Kabul. Their mission is to assess and train the local Afghan prison officers, to teach them how to run a prison without the usual corruption, death, and extortion, using some modern practices.

We move around in two B6 armoured Excursions. I keep the 'clients' in the front vehicle, while the CAT (Counter Attack Team) car follows behind. The prison is about a 45-minute drive from our base, along the Jalalabad Road, the main stretch through Kabul.

When we reach the prison entrance, they usually let us through the gates quickly. But occasionally, there's some new guard at the gate who insists we open the door for a chat. That's a hard *NO*. I usually just smile and, in my best Scottish accent, tell him to 'fuck off.'

Walking through the prison is unsettling, to say the least. The place is a maze of concrete, dimly lit corridors, broken lights, and crumbling walls. The air is thick with the stench of sweat and decay, a constant reminder of the misery within these walls. Heavy metal doors line the hallways, some barely hanging on their hinges, others bolted shut, their surfaces scarred and rusting. Each footstep echoes through the cold, narrow spaces, amplified by the silence that grips the prison. You can feel the eyes on you even before you see the faces, those of Al-Qaeda and Taliban prisoners, packed behind bars, staring you down. They look at us with this mix of hatred and curiosity, like wolves sizing up their prey. It's not just a look; it's a threat. And they know it goes both ways.

I make eye contact with a few of them as I walk through, and it's like an unspoken challenge. They can tell just by the way I carry myself that, given half a chance, I'd happily put an end to the lot of them. And I know they're thinking the same thing. If they had a moment of freedom, even just for a second, they'd slit my throat without hesitation. You can practically feel the violence hanging in the air, a razor-thin line that keeps us separated.

The tension in those hallways is suffocating. It's a place where you're never quite sure if something is about to kick off. Every glance exchanged is a reminder that, outside these walls, we'd be sworn enemies, fighting to the death. But here, in this grim, confined space, we're forced into this twisted stand-off, eyeing each other up as we go about our business.

The Exercise

Gaz and I were tasked with facilitating a training exercise for a group of non-governmental organisations who were setting foot in Kabul for the first time. These people had no clue, completely oblivious to the dangers they could face here. The boss told us to make up a scenario and make it as realistic as possible, to shake them out of their comfort zone and open their eyes to the reality of the situation.

We planned every detail meticulously, laying out scenarios that could easily happen in the chaos of Kabul. We even roped in some of the local Afghan guys to play their part. They agreed to help, though I'm not entirely sure they grasped just how intense their roles were going to be.

They were all gathered in a large room at our HQ, sitting through presentations and getting comfortable, completely unaware of what was about to unfold. Then, without warning, 'BOOM!', we tossed in a flashbang. Chaos erupted. Gaz and I dressed as local militia with AKs, faces covered, stormed in amidst the smoke and noise. The room filled with screams, and people scrambled to hide under tables, ducking behind chairs, anything to shield themselves.

Amidst the chaos, we grabbed three of them off the floor, yanking them up by their arms. They struggled and shouted, but it was no use. We quickly cuffed their hands behind their backs and shoved sacks over their heads. The panic in the room was palpable; this was exactly the kind of shock we wanted to drive home the seriousness of their situation here.

We dragged them outside and threw them into a minibus. We told the driver to just drive around the complex a bit just to get them disorientated. They were then roughly handled out and put into a room right next to where we took them and told to kneel and face the wall. There was a radio in the background just blasting out white noise and nothing was said.

One by one, we dragged them into the makeshift interrogation room, pushing their emotions right to the brink. The goal was simple: make them feel the sheer terror of a real abduction. We started with the old trick, letting them catch a whiff of petrol from a water bottle, then quickly pouring plain water over them while threatening to set them alight. It was just the beginning. Soon, they were face-to-face with our Afghan helpers, who played their part perfectly, shouting, cocking their weapons, and screaming 'Allahu Akbar' with enough fury to make anyone's blood run cold.

We didn't hold them for long, maybe a couple of hours, just enough to ensure the lesson sank in. Eventually, we shouted, 'ENDEX!' and led them back to the classroom. I must admit, I felt a twinge of sympathy for them; they were visibly shaken. But it worked. They all left that room with a newfound understanding of what to do, and more importantly, what not to do, in a conflict zone.

The Aftermath

We've just been informed that our exercise has stirred up some anger among the locals. Apparently, they feel insulted, claiming we disrespected them by portraying them as terrorists. I just don't get it. We had spoken to them beforehand, explained it was just a training exercise, and they had agreed to help us. They were all in on it, so why the sudden backlash?

Apparently, the 'Commander' is furious as well and has now turned against us. We're trying to explain the situation to him, and the boss has made it clear that this was just a training exercise and in no way intended to represent our local allies. It was never about them, but the message doesn't seem to be sinking in. Now, we're left to deal with the fallout and hope this mess can be smoothed over.

Everywhere Gaz and I go, the local guards greet us with cold, hostile stares. We try to brush it off, act like it's no big deal, but it's hard to ignore. At the end of the day, we depend on these guys to fight alongside us if things go sideways. The tension is thick, and it's a stark reminder of how quickly loyalties can shift out here.

The Boss has handed us new assignments. Gaz is being sent to Mazar, while I'm heading to Herat to set up camps with our team. Our job is to get everything ready for the State Department clients, who will be coming up to do the same work they did with the prisons here, training the locals and trying to establish some order. It's another round of the same mission, just in a different place, but this time, we'll be dealing with a whole new set of challenges.

We roll into HQ in the morning as usual, gear in tow, bug, out bags, weapons, and some scoff to get us through the day. I step outside for a smoke while waiting for the final details on the move. After a few minutes, I head back inside and reach into my bag for something. That's when I realize my pass is gone. Panic hits me instantly. It had everything, bug-out money, around $1,000, IDs, and most importantly, my passport.

This isn't right. That doesn't leave my grab bag. I never lose track of it, ever. How the hell could it just disappear? Something feels off.

I told the boss I recon one of these local bastards have stolen my gear. Word gets around fast amongst the locals, and everyone is saying the same thing, they know nothing!

Gaz is out on a detail so I can't speak to him till he returns, it feels like them against us now.

Gaz pulls in around 1600hrs and I tell him what's happened, he goes back to the house and guess what, yep, his stuff is missing too.

A couple of days pass and I am almost ready to head north, so I call the British Embassy to organise a new temp. passport.

I tell them I need paperwork when she stops me and said . . . 'Scott, you and Gaz have to come to the Embassy immediately'.

The Embassy just received intel that the Taliban have both Gaz's and my details, and they've put a bounty on our heads. I knew it! It must be the 'Commander'. I called the Boss right away, and he didn't sound surprised. 'Get back to HQ,' he ordered. 'We need to assess the situation and figure out our next move.'

I told the embassy staff that I'm not too bothered about the bounty. We're a target out here nearly every bloody day, what's new? But their reply stopped me cold. *This isn't your usual threat, Mr White.'*

Next thing I know, I'm in a long chat with the Foreign Office suits. Turns out there's a hefty price tag on both Gaz and I. Apparently, while we've been going about our day trying to blend in, we've had a couple of Special Forces lads keeping tabs on us for our safety. And if things kicked off badly, there was even an extraction plan in place to get us out of the country. That part they told me last, like an afterthought.

Now my boss has warned me, keep a low profile. So, when I'm moving about town, I wear local clothes, keep the vest off, and drive a battered old Afghan car. Just another face in the crowd. Only when I'm back on task do I switch back into normal rig.

Lying here at night in a dodgy bed behind paper, thin walls, I can't help but think… what if the Taliban kick that door in? What if tonight's the night they drag me out and put me through the same shit we practised during the old hostage scenarios, except this time it's not pretend. This time it's the real thing.

I have a RPK – a Russian belt-fed machine gun. a shotgun, AK and a pistol in my room, two facing the door and two the window at all times. If the fuckers do get in, I want to be able to fight back!

This low-life 'Commander' seems to have his hand in all sorts of dodgy dealings. He's got friends in high places, including the head of airport security, and even some connections in the government. It's becoming clear that he wants us out so he can bring in his own men. He's a ruthless bastard, and he'll do it in such a sneaky way that no one will notice until it's too late.

George has suggested we head up north a bit earlier than planned, let things cool down in Kabul for a while. Maybe if we're out of sight, they'll think we've already left the country. For now, though, we're in lockdown, no missions and no movement outside the safety of the two houses.

My old pal Bob from Iraq called me last week asking if there was any work over here, I spoke to George and told him about Bob, and how I would vouch for him as a good operator. He said there was a position available as a training instructor for the Embassy staff, and just like that we were back together, old muckers in the thick of it again.

We're sitting in the house on the sofa smoking and shooting the shit when the boss walks past, George is flying out to Khost today, and just as he's leaving, he hands me his trusted Beretta 92F. 'Nice piece,' he says casually, 'Keep an eye on that for me, I'll get it back off you in a few days.'

But George never came back for his pistol. His helicopter went down somewhere over the mountains; no one's sure if it was shot down or just a tragic accident. Everyone at HQ is feeling it, he was one of the good guys, respected by everyone who knew him. I didn't spend a huge amount of time with George, but every moment I did was enough to know he was genuine. A decent guy through and through. It's always the good ones.

I'm on the roof, sunbathing and puffing away, doing my best to smoke myself into an early grave, when my phone rings. It's HQ. The tone is grim. A US Humvee has just ploughed into a civilian taxi in the heart of the city, killing everyone inside, including a woman and a child. The fallout is immediate and ugly, the locals are going ballistic.

Every loudspeaker in the city is wailing out orders to take up arms. Riots are breaking out everywhere, and the military has decided to lock down in their camps and let this storm pass. Great. Now we're caught right in the middle of it all.

Our bases are scattered across the city, and the order comes down: gather every weapon we can and fortify ourselves on the roof. I grab my Union Jack flag, haul it up to the roof, and weigh it down with bricks. If things go sideways, we might need help if the choppers deploy.

I'm up there, crouching behind three-foot railings, staring out at the chaos unfolding below. Fires are blazing in the distance, smoke billows into the sky, and the noise of gunfire, explosions, the roar of the crowd is all around. It's utter destruction. Our bases are all in communication, calling out positions and warnings as we watch locals in a frenzy, firing RPGs into neighbouring buildings. There's a sea of them down there, hundreds, all tooled up and spoiling for a fight. It's like watching a powder keg waiting for a spark.

So here I am, ready for anything. I've got 100 smokes, my shades, a Russian RPK belt, fed machine gun, an AK-47, an MP5 submachine gun, a handful of grenades, and enough water to last through the night if it comes to that. I can hear the crackle of static over the radio, updates flying in from the other bases. Everyone is on edge, scanning their sectors. We know the drill, hold the high ground, maintain comms, and be ready to fight like hell if they come for us.

I look around at the other lads on the roof; we're all in our own worlds, focused, we've been in tight spots before, but this feels different. It's not just another skirmish; it's a full-blown city uprising. I light another cigarette, squinting through the haze of smoke and heat. If they come, we'll be ready. But for now, it's a waiting game.

Six hours have passed and it looks like it's all calming down, thank fuck, I'm starving! Got a good t-shirt tan though.

Herat

I'm up in Herat now after catching a UN flight, I'm in this tiny wee Conex in a US military camp with AC and a bed, that's it for now, not too bad

We're outside an Italian Special Forces camp and we can get in to buy food and shit from their shop, it's full of cheese, and fucking wine, not a decent sausage roll or Fray Bentos pie here!? The lads here all look like they've just stepped off a catwalk, neat stubble, Ray-Bans, and a cigarette casually hanging from their mouths.

At 1900 hrs, I get a call from Kabul, telling me the Taliban have pinpointed our location and are coming for us. My gut reaction is a surge of adrenaline. 'Alright,' I think, 'fuck it, bring it on.' But as the reality sets in, I realise it's not just my life on the line here. If they come, they won't just be targeting me; they'll go after my team and clients too. And that's a risk I can't justify.

I start on a few vodkas and light up a fat cigar before picking up the phone to call Gaz over in Mazar. We start talking through our options, our heads clouded with the booze. One idea is to bug out, Gaz could try to make a run for the border into Tajikistan while I'd head east towards Iran. It seemed like a good plan at the time.

But as the hours tick by, and we sober up in the morning light, reality hits us. It was a shit idea. A half-baked plan born out of adrenalin and vodka. We both know fleeing on our own would just put us in more danger. The risk is too great, the escape routes too uncertain. So, we scrap the plan and decide to regroup, hoping to come up with something better. I call HQ who have spoken to the British Embassy, they said if we can get to them, they will ensure our safe passage out of the country.

I pop in to see the Italians and casually ask if they've got any military flights heading to Kabul. By sheer luck, they have one scheduled to go in 24 hours. Perfect. Without wasting a second,

I pack up all my gear, label it to be sent back to the UK, and prepare for the move. Now, all I can do is wait.

The flight into Kabul feels tense, but it's the ride back that really gets my heart pounding. As soon as we land, I'm bundled into the back seat of a vehicle, a blanket thrown over me for cover. We're speeding through the streets of Kabul, heading towards the safety of the embassy. This is my world now, ducking, dodging, and hoping to make it to the next checkpoint in one piece or fight to the death trying.

I'm in the Embassy now when a tall guy steps into the room and lays out the plan. 'Here's the deal... no military flights heading out for a few days, so we're getting you on a civilian flight instead. But we can't go through the usual channels, the airport security has all your details, thanks to the Commander, and they'd have you picked up right away.'

So, the plan is to sneak me in airside. Same drill, back seat, blanket thrown over me, hidden from view until we reach the stairs of a plane bound for Dubai. It's all cloak, and, dagger, but it's my best shot.

I'm sitting here, in the back of the car, the plane is in sight, and the stairs are down, waiting for the nod to run. Adrenaline rushing, 'Right, go now!' Without a second thought, I sprint up the stairs and duck into the plane, quickly grab a seat at the rear. *Thank fuck that's over*, I think, *get me a bloody drink.*

The doors close, and I let out a sigh of relief, starting to relax. But then, out of nowhere, the front doors fly open. A massive Afghan military officer steps in, his eyes scanning up and down the rows of seats. *Fuck, this is it. I'm busted.* My mind races, I'm either facing years in some shit hole jail or I'm getting handed over to the Taliban.

He stops about four rows ahead; eyes locked on some guy. My heart is beating so fast I'm thinking I'm not going without a fight. The officer suddenly snaps to attention, salutes the man, shakes his hand, then walks off the plane. I can't believe what just happened. *You can't make this shit up.* My nerves are shot to shit, where's that drink!

I touch down in Dubai and call Sarah just to say it's over, I am picked up from the airport and taken to a hotel for the night before heading back home.

Bevan was set to fly out on leave today, but things took a turn for the worse. While I'm in Dubai, I get a call from one of the lads back in Kabul. 'Bevan's been taken,' he says. 'Taken? Taken where, and by who?' I asked, I could feel the anger rising inside me.

It turns out that bastard Commander planted drugs inside a tub of protein powder!!

Bevan had the option to travel on a United Nations charter plane, which would have by passed airport security, but he chose to go with a civilian airline. If he were actually guilty of smuggling drugs, why on earth would he opt for the more scrutinized route? It didn't make sense. That sneaky, horrible bastard Commander with all his connections . . . He couldn't get Gaz or me, so he went after Bevan instead.

He's been handed over to the Afghan authorities, that's all we know for now.

Chapter 11

Aegis Defence

After a few months of well-deserved leave, I've decided it's time to see who else is hiring. Col. Tim Spicer has a superb company in Iraq called Aegis Defence. They're massive, well-equipped, professional, and they pay well. So, I'm heading back down to London for a meeting with them.

This time around, I'm not as green as I was when I first started out. I've spent a few years in conflict zones, and I know what I'm getting into. Still, I can't help but feel a surge of excitement at the thought of getting back in the saddle, back in the thick of it with good blokes and a company that knows how to do things right.

September 2006

Landing in Baghdad on a C-130, weaving through combat manoeuvres, I'm reminded of where I truly belong. The scent of aviation fuel fills my lungs, mingling with the heat that hits me the moment I step off the ramp. The chaotic noises, shouts, engines, distant gunfire, they're all strangely comforting now, almost like I'm home.

A team of blokes picks me up, and straight away, I notice the difference from previous outfits. These guys are kitted out properly, they're wearing Nomex fireproof flight suits, solid, top-tier body armour, and their vehicles are impressive, top American Humvees and Excursions, kitted out with rear gunner seats and portholes for firing positions, Not like before when if we needed to shoot from our cars, we would just roll the window down or fire through the doors.

This feels professional, well-equipped. It's reassuring, and for the first time in a while, I feel like I'm exactly where I need to be.

We make our way down 'Route Irish', currently the most dangerous stretch of road in the world. It's an eight-mile gauntlet from the airport to the Green Zone, and it's a hotspot for insurgent attacks. Every day, this road gets hammered, ambushes, IEDs, and gunfire, turning each trip into a gamble. The US military is constantly patrolling, trying to keep it under control, but despite their efforts, there are still incidents here every single day. When I was here last, we would run this route in low profile vehicles, blending in as not to draw attention. Now, we're running high profile with signs on the vehicles in both English and Arabic saying 'Stay back 100m or you will be shot'. This has come about as too many times suicide bombers would drive their cars into teams and wipe them out.

We've got new rules of engagement now. If a vehicle gets too close, the rear CAT car waves an orange flag out of the porthole as a warning. If that's ignored, we launch a flare at them. Still no response? We put rounds into the engine block. And if they're still not complying, we aim for the windshield. But here's the thing, it can all change in a heartbeat. Sometimes, a vehicle comes barrelling up too fast, and you just know it's a car bomb. In those cases, there's no time for warnings; you take out the threat immediately.

I can't believe how much the place has changed. I haven't been here in over six months, and now Baghdad is complete chaos. It's one massive war zone, corpses line the streets, burnt-out cars scattered everywhere, while US tanks and Explosive Ordnance Disposal teams are constantly patrolling. The level of violence and destruction is unreal.

Despite the carnage outside, our setup here is impressive. We're in the middle of the Green Zone, living in chalet blocks, two-storey rows shared with the US military. These guys know how to establish a camp; there's a PX (American shop), a Burger King, Pizza Hut, and even Green Beans Coffee houses. It's a far cry from the ration packs we were scraping by on not so long ago.

Of course, being in such a high-profile area comes with its own risks. We're under constant attack from mortars and rockets, usually launched from Sadr City, just outside the Green Zone. We have an Early warning system called CRAM, Counter Rocket Artillery and Mortar which senses incoming through radar then you hear a siren blaring first, followed by 'Incoming, incoming! Seek shelter!' You're supposed to run to the nearest concrete bunker, but sometimes that's not an option. In those moments, all you can do is close your eyes, brace yourself, and hope like hell it misses you.

My job here is a member of the SET Teams (Security Escort Team). We run with three high profile heavily armoured 4x4s.

Our primary role out here is to protect the American Military Corps of Engineers, US officials, along with high-ranking Colonels and Generals who are constantly moving through high-threat zones. These aren't routine escorts. These are high-value targets in one of the deadliest operational theatres on Earth.

I've landed in a good squad now with this mob, Swordfish 3. Decent outfit. Ten-man team, all internationals plus one local interpreter. No weak links, everyone's switched on.

When anyone new starts with Aegis, they've got to go through a week of pre-deployment training and assessment. It's not just ticking boxes either, it's a proper shakeout. You're pushed through drills, Fitness assessments, hit the range to prove you can shoot straight, polish up your trauma skills, then you're thrown behind the wheel of a 25-ton armoured SUV. Just to put that into perspective, that's around ten times heavier than your average 4x4. It's like driving a tank through tight streets, and they expect you to handle it like a rally car.

The structure is pretty standard, Team Leader in the first vehicle, the second normally has your principle then the CAT (Counter attack team) is the rear vehicle with the second in command, everyone rotates roles depending on the tasking. One day you're driving point in the lead wagon, next day you're in the back vehicle with loads of Gucci kit as rear gunner. No one's static, and that's how it should be, keeps you sharp.

There's an unspoken rule though, well, not so unspoken anymore. If you've had a few incidents while covering the rear, you get rotated out. Doesn't matter if you're the best shot in the convoy, they don't want one bloke stacking up statistics. It's not about skill, it's about optics. If the higher-ups ever come poking around, it looks bad on paper if one guy's involved in all the shooting incidents. Makes it look like it's personal.

So, they move us around. Keeps it even. Keeps the questions away. War by the book, apparently.

We ran all kinds of missions as part of the SET team but nothing about the job felt standard. Our primary task was to escort high, ranking military personnel and civilian officials all over Baghdad. These weren't your average foot soldiers, these were Colonels, and Government advisors, the kind of men and women who walked into a meeting and changed the course of operations with a single order.

Our destinations ranged from secure Government ministries and military HQs to chaotic construction sites and vulnerable infrastructure hubs like power stations or water facilities. Every single location came with its own unique threat level. Some we only visited once. Others, unfortunately, became repeat destinations. That's when the tension really kicked in. The more often we ran the same route, the more we risked falling into a pattern. And in this place, patterns meant death.

Baghdad wasn't just hostile, it was intelligent. The enemy watched. They waited. Every time we left the gate; we had to assume someone had clocked us. It only took one slip-up, one route repeated too often, one schedule too predictable, and they'd have us boxed in and lit up before we even saw it coming.

To stay alive, we had to adapt constantly. Routes were changed daily. No straight paths, no routine. One day we'd sweep through

Karada in the early morning, the next we'd cut in late afternoon through back alleys near the Green Zone wall or take a detour along the edge of Sadr City if there was no other option. Every road felt like it was holding its breath. The planning that went into each run was meticulous, but it was necessary to keep from being ambushed.

People think we were just armed chauffeurs, babysitting brass from one air-conditioned room to another. They've no idea. Out there, we weren't just drivers/operators, we were the barrier between a successful mission and a massacre. And every time we rolled out, we did it knowing full well it could be our last.

Mac's the Team Leader of SF3. Big Black lad, ex-Sergeant in the Guards, Lean and muscular and looks like he walked straight off the set of *Blade*. Always confident. He's got us all doing compulsory PT most afternoons, circuits, bodyweight drills. Not really my thing, to be honest. I've always been more of a weights man, bars, plates, and serious iron. But fair play to him, cardio's got its place out here. Keeps the lungs working and the edge sharp when you need to leg it under fire I suppose.

Mark: ex-Marine, Wee wiry guy in his early 30s, curly mop of hair and a face like he's permanently pissed off. Always mouthing off, always got someone to slag. You never know when he's going to whip his knob out either, usually at the worst possible time.

Boyle's another good lad. Ex-Para. Early 30s, good head, good heart. Always happy, likes a laugh but calm under pressure. No drama, no ego, just dependable.

Jo, our resident South African. Mostly sticks to driving. Bit of a know-it-all if I'm honest. Talks a lot of nonsense, always has the 'better way' of doing things, even when nobody's asked. But when it kicks off, he can throw that wagon around like a rally car, and that's worth more than his mouth.

Knoll was our 2IC. Young lad, ex-Para sniper. Sound, quiet, switched on, carried himself well under pressure. I actually had a lot of time for him. Trusted him. Thought he had potential but unfortunately I found out he had a face for everyone and to me he was Judas.

Then there's **Jason**: another Marine, this one from Manchester. Top bloke. Been there, seen it, got the scars to prove it. Took an IED blast a while back, lucky to be breathing. Spent nine months recovering, and instead of packing it in, he came straight back out here to carry on. Different breed. The Yanks even gave him a medal for it – *The Defence of Freedom Medal*. I remember him getting presented it, face beetroot red. Knowing Jason, it probably went straight into the bottom of his gorilla box, buried under socks and lad's mags. Never been one for the spotlight.

Then there's me, the only Scottish bloke, so I was obviously nicknamed 'Jock'.

So that's the team, a patchwork of personalities, backgrounds, and battle scars, all thrown together in one of the most dangerous places on the planet.

What could possibly go wrong?

Some of the places we go, we're met with open hostility. You can feel it before you even step out of the vehicle, eyes on you, the weight of silent hatred pressing in from all directions. Just the other day we were visiting the Ministry of Interior. We were escorting a high-level client to a meeting, routine enough on paper, but the air in that building was thick with resentment. As we stood in the corridor waiting, I could hear Iraqi militia music blaring from a cheap mobile phone in one of the nearby offices. Proper hate fuel, the kind of stuff insurgents play before they strap on a vest.

You don't need anyone to say a word. The stares say it all. Pure contempt. They look at us like invaders, like we're the enemy, completely oblivious, or just not willing to accept, that we're here trying to keep their country from tearing itself apart.

That day, I decided to push the boundary a bit. Maybe it was the tension, maybe I just wanted to look the devil in the eye. I walked straight into the guy's office, the one with the music, and with a cigarette hanging out my mouth and my hand ready to draw my Glock, I casually asked him for a light. He looked up, surprised but not aggressive. Lit my smoke and asked in broken English where I was from.

'Scotland,' I said.

Something shifted in the room. His whole face changed – like I'd flipped a switch.

'Ahh . . . Scotland!' he said, breaking into a grin. 'William Wallace! Braveheart!' Then he followed it up with a smirk: 'Scotland good . . . England no good.'

And just like that, I'd apparently made a connection. Maybe he saw us as fellow underdogs, two nations with their own history of resistance. He went on to say, 'IRA good!' as if lumping us all into one basket of freedom fighters.

It was strange, hearing that, but not surprising. Over here, the lines between terrorist and hero are blurred, depending on which side of the suffering you're on. And to be honest, with everything going on in Iraq, the bloodshed, the corruption, the foreign boots on their streets, I couldn't entirely blame him. Maybe in his eyes, we weren't that different after all.

Now, don't get me wrong, the company I'm with is first class. The kit is top-notch, the training is decent, and the pay reflects the danger. On paper, it's a great outfit. But here's the harsh truth: none of that matters when the enemy doesn't care who you are or how well you're geared up. The rules of engagement mean nothing when you're on a street riddled with IEDs or driving past a mob with RPGs tucked under their jackets.

The risks now are off the chart. We're losing men daily. Some to ambushes, some to random roadside bombs, and others just caught in the wrong place at the wrong time. And it's not just the casualties, guys are resigning left, right, and centre.

There's a growing sense that it's no longer *if* something happens, it's *when*. We all feel it. We joke about it, dark humour being the only thing holding sanity together, but deep down, the truth's gnawing at everyone. We're not counting days anymore, we're counting chances. At this rate, it feels like it's only a matter of time before we're shipped home in body bags. This job might have started out with pride and purpose, but now it's pure adrenalin-packed mayhem.

We were tasked with moving a VIP into a ministerial building in the city. On paper it was routine. We were running Route Pluto, a stretch that had been taking hits for days. Insurgents liked it. Which meant I didn't.

I was in the rear vehicle, 'Charlie', our standard setup. The lead with Mac upfront and the VIP in the middle car. The comms carried the usual running commentary from 'Alpha'. Anything that looked out of place got called early. Parked cars. Roadkill. Loose rubble. You learn to spot the small details.

The road was almost empty. One or two cars at most on a highway that was normally rammed. Locals don't avoid a route without a reason; the question is always the same, what do they know that we don't?

Alpha came over the net. Police station on the right. Five Iraqi Police on the roof. We spotted them just standing smoking, chatting and watching the road?

Ten seconds later the road disappeared.

The blast hit Alpha hard. A massive IED. Smoke and debris swallowed the lead and the VIP vehicle as rocks smashed into us. We drove straight through the cloud and saw both vehicles ahead were still moving. Quick comms check, waiting for the follow-up. The small arms. The secondary device. The final nail.

It never came.

One by one the calls went out. Alpha okay. Bravo okay. Charlie okay.

The IED had done enough damage to remind us it was there, shredding the outer glass on Mac's vehicle, lifted it off the road slightly, but the armour held. B6 doing exactly what it was paid to do. The tyres and wheels were all still intact and they could still drive.

We sent the grid back to base, reported contact, did a rapid assessment and took an alternative route back to base to get patched up.

When the radio finally went quiet, I said what everyone was thinking.
'Cheeky fuckers!

Jason snorted. ' Those fucking Police I bet ya.'

There is a new type of roadside bomb Al-Qaeda are using over here, it's called an EFP – Explosively Formed Projectile. Sounds technical, but trust me, it's pure fucking evil. It's a shaped charge, usually buried roadside in some pile of rubble or fake curb, rigged up with wires or a passive infra-red sensor. When it goes off, it doesn't just explode, it fires a molten slug of copper at supersonic speed. It punches through armour like it's paper. Doesn't matter if you're in a 30-ton tank or an armoured SUV, if an EFP hits you clean, you're gone. The front end of your vehicle turns into a furnace, the inside becomes a blender, and you're lucky if there's anything left to bag up. These things were designed with one purpose, to kill Westerners. And they're bloody good at it.

To deal with EFPs, we'd rig up something called a Rhino – a simple bit of kit, but it could save lives. It's basically a long metal arm welded to the front of the vehicle with a heat source, usually just a toaster element or glow plug, fixed to the end of it. Sounds daft, but here's how it works: EFPs are often triggered by passive infra-red sensors. They're looking for heat, like the engine block of your vehicle.

So, the Rhino gives them something hotter, but a few feet out in front. Idea is, the EFP fires early, before it's lined up with your cab. Instead of sending a molten slug straight through your chest, it smashes into the dirt or blows the front grille off. Not perfect. Not guaranteed. But it could give us a fighting chance. And out there, that's all you could ask for.

22 October 2006

Got some really shit news today. Seb Cullen from my old outfit was killed last night.

Seb and I were out here around the same time, one of the lads who knew what this life really meant. It's starting to feel like all the old sweats are getting picked off one by one. You spend years pushing your luck out here, and deep down you know it can't last forever. But hearing it actually happen again and again . . . Shit.

Seb was taken out by an EFP, the blast ripped through the vehicle and sent it up in flames. The guys with him, helpless, they couldn't get close. All they could do was stand there and watch. Christ . . . what a fucking way to go. No one deserves that. No chance to fight back, no final words, just fire and steel and silence.

It's moments like this that shake you. I've said it before, I know there's a time when you've got to walk away from this life, before it takes everything. Maybe I've already stayed too long. I hate this part... burying mates in your head, again and again, and wondering if your name's the next one passed around the camp.

Rest easy, Seb. You were one of the good ones.

5 November 2006

Today's the day Saddam gets his verdict. We're on full lockdown inside the Green Zone, no movement in or out. The courthouse is just a stone's-throw from where we're based, and the tension in the air is thick. You can feel it, something's coming.

It's been eerily quiet in Baghdad the last couple of days. No gunfire, no roadside bombs, hardly a whisper. That's never a good sign out here. It usually means they're regrouping, stockpiling weapons, and waiting for the right moment to unleash hell. And if Saddam's sentenced to death, which we all expect, there's going to be carnage. Massive bloodshed. No question.

What makes it even more surreal is the date. 5th of November, Guy Fawkes Night. The day he tried to blow up the English Parliament and ended up getting burned for it. Now, hundreds of years later, we're sitting in a war zone waiting to see if another man meets the same fate. Different country, different century . . . same fire in the powder keg.

Funny how history repeats itself. Except here, it's not fireworks in the sky we're expecting, it's mortars and body parts.

Here's an article from Reuters today:

Saddam to hear fate, Iraq in tense lockdown
BAGHDAD (Reuters). With Saddam Hussein hours from learning whether he will hang, Iraq's government, imposed curfews on Sunday and has cancelled army leave, fearing the historic trial verdict might trigger fresh sectarian bloodletting.

As Baghdad went into lockdown overnight, mortars slammed into the mainly Sunni district of Adhamiya, killing seven people and wounding 20, an Interior Ministry source.

Prime Minister Nuri al-Maliki, who called for the ousted president to be executed quickly, said he should get 'what he deserves' for killing, torturing or jailing hundreds of Shi'ite Muslims after gunmen from Maliki's Shi'ite Dawa party tried to kill Saddam in the town of Dujail in 1982.

'If he is guilty, he deserves the death penalty,' Ali Hassan, who testified against Saddam last year, told Reuters in Dujail. 'The law must take its course.'

Chief judge Raouf Abdul Rahman, an ethnic Kurd, was expected to summon the court to order from around 10 a.m. (0700 GMT) and spend several hours delivering a summary of the verdicts and sentences for Saddam and seven others accused of crimes against humanity, though court officials do not rule out a postponement.

A full text of the five judges' rulings, running to hundreds of pages, will be issued in the coming days, court sources said.

A death sentence or life imprisonment generates an automatic appeal, delaying any execution by months at least. Saddam, with rhetoric typical of his defence over the past year, has told the court he wants to face a military firing squad, not the hangman.

LOCKDOWN

Baghdad went into total curfew overnight, as did Saddam's home province, including Dujail, and other areas where fellow minority Sunni Arabs could hit back at a guilty verdict.

Yet an embryonic civil war that is killing hundreds of people a week has left many Iraqis indifferent to the fate of the 69-year-old fallen strongman as he has argued theatrically for his life at the courthouse in one of his Baath party's old buildings in the heavily fortified, US, protected Green Zone.

The killing of three defence counsel, fearful witnesses and a chief judge who quit over government interference has also tarnished the credibility of one of the great experiments in the law of war crimes since Nazi leaders were tried at Nuremberg 60 years ago.

After Saddam's capture three years ago, the American occupiers resisted calls for the case to be handed over to an international court such as those for Rwanda and the former Yugoslavia. Instead, they said, Iraqis should try Saddam themselves and in the process exorcise 30 years of fear.

Yet the violence that erupted once Saddam's oppression was lifted has threatened to engulf the Iraqi High Tribunal.

Funded, trained and heavily guided at times by American lawyers, the special court has so far launched two trials – the second a genocide prosecution over the deaths of 180,000 Kurds in 1988 – and has up to a dozen other cases in the works.

Prosecutors have sought death sentences for Saddam, his half-brother and former intelligence chief Barzan al-Tikriti, vice president Taha Yassin Ramadan and judge Awad al-Bander. Three minor Baath party officials from Dujail also face sentencing while a fourth has been recommended for acquittal.

Nine men were killed immediately after the assassination bid on July 8, 1982. Another 148, some of whom had already died under torture, were later sentenced to death by Bander. Saddam said he ordered the executions and justified them because those killed were agents of Shi'ite Iran, with which Iraq was at war.

Human rights activists have criticised the quality of the casework and the court's difficulties in protecting witnesses and defence lawyers. Its proponents point to a substantial body of evidence, gripping witness testimony on torture and killing and accuse Saddam's attorneys of shambolic grandstanding.

Saddam's defenders denounce the trial as 'victor's justice'. One of them, former US Attorney General Ramsey Clark, said hanging him could 'create violence . . . for generations to come'.

However, Saddam's ability to rouse passions in the nation he subdued for three decades seems to have diminished since Iraqis first watched in awe as, now bearded and a prisoner, he told the court on its first day a year ago: 'I am the president of Iraq.'

Tuesday 17 April

This morning 0500hrs just like most mornings, I rolled out of bed, jumped in the shower, same routine as always. But just as the water hit my face, I heard a load of shouting outside my room, panic in the voices, the kind you instantly know isn't just lads messing about.

I grabbed a towel and stepped out to see what was going on.

Death's a daily thing here, you build up a sort of numbness to it. It's just background noise in a place like this. But today hit different. A young American soldier in the next bunk to me decided to end it all. Shot himself in the head.

I helped smash in the door and when we got inside, he was still alive, barely breathing but still had a pulse. The scene was chaos, blood and brains splattered across the walls. I remember slipping on a lump of it as we tried to get him onto the stretcher. One of the guys was trying to keep his skull together while we moved him out. The medics had arrived at this point and rushed him across to the hospital, only 200 yards away but he was gone by the time they got him through the doors.

Turns out he phoned his wife back in the States, told her what he was about to do. She panicked and rang one of his mates over here, but by the time he made it to the room, it was already done.

Poor lad left behind a young wife and five kids. Five bloody kids.

I don't know what to say about it. He was a clerk – word going around was he'd been skimming a few quid here and there, got caught, and couldn't face the fallout. So, he took the only way out he could see.

A stupid, brutal waste of a life. And now another family back home gets the knock on the door.

Wednesday 18 April 2007

We've lost three men this week, three in seven days, all taken out by EFPs. Even the Rhino kit fails sometimes.

Today, it was Jack and Les from SET 5. Their armoured 4x4 didn't stand a chance. The bastards timed the explosion perfectly. The EFP tore through the vehicle like it was paper. Jack was ripped clean in half. Les was barely recognisable, just a mess of flesh and twisted limbs. A US Colonel riding with them had both his legs blown clean off. Carnage doesn't even begin to describe it.

Once the dust settled, the lads who were following behind tried everything to get into the wreckage. The blast had jammed the doors, and the ballistic glass held firm, too strong to smash by hand. They grabbed the emergency axe we keep in the back of all vehicles and went to work on the front windscreen. It took everything they had to break through and crawl inside.

There was nothing they could do for Jack or Les. It was over for them in seconds. But the Colonel . . . he was still clinging on. They said he was unconscious, barely breathing, with this horrible gurgling sound coming from his throat. Blood was pumping out from the stumps where his legs used to be. Dave managed to get tourniquets on both legs, trying desperately to slow the bleed and stabilise him. But it was no good. He slipped away not long after.

What hits hardest is how fast it all happens. I was talking to Jack maybe an hour before they rolled out. We were chatting about home, about his wife and kids back in the UK. Laughing one minute . . . and an hour later, he's gone. Just like that. His family has no clue their world is about to be shattered. It always brings things crashing back down how fragile this life is.

Now I've been tasked with stepping in to replace Jack in SET 5. Two days after the hit, and I'm walking into a team that's broken. You can see it in their eyes, dead behind the stare. Some of the lads have gone home, couldn't take it after seeing what was left of their mates. Others stayed, mostly out of stubbornness or because they don't know what else to do. In my opinion, the whole team should've been pulled out for rest, given time to breathe. But no. They decided to stay until they go on leave.

That's the reality. Unfortunately, we're replaceable. Bodies for contracts. Doesn't matter what we've seen, what we carry with us, or what we've just had to scrape off the dashboard of a burning truck. If there's still a seat to fill, someone's getting thrown in it.

And this week, that someone's me.

After the latest incident and some of the lads eventually going home, we've all been told we're getting evaluated for PTSD – Post Traumatic Stress Disorder. No surprise there. They marched us over to the American hospital where the Padre was looking at us all as if we all lost our mothers.

We were handed self-assessment forms, tick boxes and rating scales. 'How often do you feel anxious?' 'Do you suffer from nightmares?' 'Have you lost interest in things you used to enjoy?' I had to laugh. I mean, come on . . . most of us are walking case studies for mental health disorders. But that's no revelation, we already knew we were fucked up. Hell, you *have* to be a bit mad to do this job in the first place.

We've all seen too much, done too much, buried too much. The only difference is some lads talk about it, and some just shove it deep down where it rots quietly. But now we're expected to tick some boxes and get a label slapped on us so they can say, 'Yeah, we're looking after their welfare.'

Just so you are aware of what's actually going on here in Baghdad, here is the latest report from Reuters:

BAGHDAD (Reuters) – Car bombs killed nearly 170 people in Baghdad on Wednesday in the deadliest attacks in the city since US and Iraqi forces launched a security crackdown aimed at halting the country's slide into civil war.

One car bomb alone in the mainly Shi'ite Sadriya neighbourhood killed 118 people and wounded 139, police said.

The apparently coordinated attacks – there were five within a short space of time – occurred hours after Shi'ite Prime Minister Nuri al-Maliki said Iraq would take security control of the whole country from foreign forces by the end of the year.

More than 200 people were wounded in total.

Sunni Islamist Al-Qaeda are blamed for most of the major bombing attacks targeting Shi'ites in Iraq.

Maliki is under growing pressure to say when US troops will leave, but the attacks in mainly Shi'ite areas of Baghdad underscored the huge security challenges.

'I saw dozens of dead bodies. Some people were burned alive inside minibuses. Nobody could reach them after the explosion,' said a Reuters witness at Sadriya, describing scenes of mayhem at an intersection where the bomb exploded near a market.

'There were pieces of flesh all over the place. Women were screaming and shouting for their loved ones who died,' said the witness who did not wish to be identified, adding many of the dead were women and children.

One man waving his arms in the air screamed hysterically: 'Where's Maliki? Let him come and see what is happening here.'

US and Iraqi forces began deploying thousands more troops onto Baghdad's streets in February.

Sectarian death squads killings have declined, but car bombs are much harder to stop, US military officials say.

The attacks could inflame sectarian passions in Baghdad, especially among the Mehdi Army militia of anti-American Shi'ite cleric Moqtada al-Sadr.

The militia, which numbers in the tens of thousands, has been keeping a low profile since the crackdown began. Washington calls the militia the greatest threat to peace in Iraq.

Sadr withdrew his six ministers from Maliki's cabinet on Monday to press for a pull-out timetable for the 146,000 US troops in Iraq.

Among the other attacks, police said a suicide car bomber killed 35 people at a checkpoint in Sadr City, the stronghold of the firebrand cleric. A third car bomb attack in the capital killed 10 people, police said.

THE EPICENTRE OF VIOLENCE

At Sadriya, television footage showed a thick, dark plume of smoke rising at the scene of the bombing. Fire fighters rushed to put out flames on burning bodies, while rescue workers tried to retrieve bodies from the blackened hulks of cars.

The Sadriya bombing was the highest death toll in a single attack in Baghdad since a truck bomb killed 135 people and wounded 305 in the same area on February 3.

Baghdad has been the epicentre of violence in Iraq since suspected Sunni Al-Qaeda militants blew up a holy Shi'ite shrine in the city of Samarra in February 2006.

In a speech at a ceremony marking the handover of southern Maysan province from British to Iraqi control,

Maliki said three provinces in the autonomous Kurdistan region would be next, followed by Kerbala and Wasit provinces.

'Then it will be province by province until we achieve (this transfer) before the end of the year,' Maliki said in the speech delivered on his behalf by National Security Adviser Mowaffaq al, Rubaie.

Maysan is the fourth of Iraq's 18 provinces to be handed to Iraqi security forces, joining Muthanna, Najaf and DhiQar, all predominantly Shi'ite and relatively calm regions in the south.

Maliki says Iraq's security forces will only take back control from foreign forces when ready, and he urged patience.

10 May 2007

Today our mission was to take a US Colonel and three of his aides to a disused building, hoping to restore it to make a youth centre for the locals. This was in the Abu Ghraib district of Baghdad. Straight away, alarm bells.

The area we were heading into was officially classed as a 'Black Route', completely off-limits to Coalition forces due to high levels of insurgent activity. Upper management said we would go, I mean, that's what we're paid for yeah? Doing things the Military won't do.

We gathered in the briefing room, reviewing the mission plan, route details, and standard operating procedures. On the surface, it all seemed structured with maps laid out, radio frequencies confirmed, contact points noted. But beneath the routine, it felt more like a formality, a box-ticking exercise designed to create the illusion that someone, somewhere, had a grip on the chaos we were walking into. As the team sat in silence, listening to the rundown, I scanned the room. You could see it on their faces everyone thinking the same thing but too professional or too numb to voice it.

So, I said what everyone else was too polite to ask:

'Just make sure my wife gets paid out the insurance when we're killed today.'

Bit of nervous laughter from the Colonel and his aides, but the kind where everyone knows it's not really a joke.

I was rear gunner on this run, perched in the back of the last vehicle, facing out. I had the M249 SAW with me, a belt-fed bastard that spits out rounds like a chainsaw on steroids. My M4 slung close, pistol at my side, smoke and flares ready to go. Two ammo boxes, 500 rounds each, rattling under my feet. My job? Simple. Don't let anything get near us.

Out here, a car getting too close isn't just a concern, it's a fucking death sentence. VBIEDs are the big one. You miss it, you don't just die, you disappear. Pink mist, scattered teeth, and silence. We rolled out early. The journey was quiet, not too long, just like another day. But as we reached the target site, that all changed.

As we approached down a dirt road, a local guard who'd been standing nearby suddenly legged it. First combat indicator, this was relayed over the radio.

The site itself was a walled-off compound, about the size of a football field. Inside, an old brick building, bullet holes, cracked walls, dust everywhere. Apparently, the US Corps of Engineers were planning to drop $3 million into restoring it for the locals. Good PR move, bad tactical one.

We pulled in and escorted the VIPs out so they could get their photos and pretend to assess the building. I took up a defensive position at a gap in the exterior wall, slung my SAW over my shoulder so I had eyes on a main road and four sets of high-rise flats across the way, all falling apart, full of holes, corners crumbling. There were a few women and kids were wandering about . . . but no men.

Then I saw it, a white saloon car tearing down the road in our direction.

Instinct kicked in. I ducked behind the wall to avoid being spotted initially, eyes on the approach. The car skidded to a halt maybe 20ft from me and I heard the doors open.

I saw three insurgents jump out. AKs and pistols. All of them in civvies, jeans, shemaghs with only their eyes showing.

'Fuck me.' It was on.

They spotted me immediately and opened fire. Rounds cracked past my head. And hit the wall I was leaning on. I flipped off the safety, swung the barrel toward them, shouted

'CONTACT LEFT' and laid down hell.

The roar of the SAW echoed through the compound like thunder.

One of them, wearing jeans, a red-checked shirt, bolted across the street toward the flats. He fired back over his shoulder, gangster style. I saw the shock in his eyes, I don't think they were expecting such a fight, Idiot. I walked my rounds into him. Watched as he folded mid-run, torn apart by 5.56mm. Dropped just before reaching cover of the building.

I turned my fire on the other two who had jumped back into the vehicle and tried to bug out while still firing out the windows. I riddled the car with the rest of the box, I reckon about 300 rounds right into it as it tried to flee, It got about 100 yards up the road before coming to a halt all fucked up, smoke pissing from it, but no movement from inside.

Just when I thought it was over, more rounds started flying in from the building's opposite. The ambush was bigger than we thought.

I popped a smoke grenade while laying down suppressive fire, the team moved to extract the clients. Once they had got clear I sprinted back under fire to the vehicles. The lads were in the process of trying to get them all into the vehicles . . .

'MOVE! MOVE!' I shouted. 'NOW FOR FUCKS SAKE!

They bolted, but the Colonel, Christ . . he just froze. Wouldn't budge. Eyes wide, hands shaking. It was like he couldn't compute what was happening. One of our lads physically pushed him forward, and as he scrambled into the SUV, he accidentally discharged his rifle. bang-bang – two shots into the air, why? Who knows?

We finally got them all into the vehicle. I jumped in the rear door and the driver had put the foot flat on the pedal . . . We tore out of there, engine screaming, tyres spitting dust. Rounds were still snapping past us, banging off the wagon but we were moving.

I was breathing hard, heart still pounding, sweat pissing down my face and soaking through my flight suit. And yet, despite the chaos, I felt it, a strange, undeniable sense of pride. We'd just faced down another full-blown ambush and lived to tell the tale.

One of the lads leaned over the seats into the back and clapped me on the back and shouted, 'Well done, Jock'.

That got a few nods and smirks. The tension started to lift as we exhaled, adrenaline still buzzing in our veins.

A few of us cracked jokes, the usual dark humour. There were chuckles here and there, that kind of awkward laughter you let out when you realise just how close you came to dying. Someone muttered something about the sheer audacity of the attack, and I couldn't help myself.

'Typical jihadi,' I said, smirking. 'Brings a knife to a gunfight.'

That one landed. The lads burst out laughing, the kind of deep, gritty laugh that breaks the tension after something close and bloody. It was a release. A reminder we were still here.

We reported back to HQ, gave them the quick version, contact, engagement, cleared out, no friendly casualties, wind, down mode slowly creeping in. Another day in Baghdad. Another ambush survived. Another memory added to the ever, growing reel of madness.

I'm heading home on leave for a couple of weeks, and yeah, I'm looking forward to it.

We usually get flown out on a Military C-130, either into Kuwait or Amman, Jordan. We stay for 24 hours in a nice hotel before heading home. First thing I do when I get there is get a proper scrub, wash the dust and stress off, then order something hot and heavy from room service. A steak and a pudding always helps. After that, I head down to the lounge bar. You always see a few familiar faces, lads on the same decompression path. You nod, share a pint or two, and just chill out in a space where no one's trying to kill you. It's calm. Safe. A strange contrast to where you've just come from.

Just landed in Edinburgh. Sarah and Kyle are there waiting at the airport, just like always. The look on Kyle's face when he sees me, God, it never gets old. His whole body lights up, and then the tears come as he bolts toward me. I always try to bring him something from the American Shop on camp – maybe a stuffed toy, or a shiny little gadget he can show his pals. Sarah kisses me, wraps her arms around me, and gives me that quiet look that says, *welcome home*, without needing the words.

There's a weight hanging over me, even when I'm supposed to be relaxing. It seems to be the same on every leave I have now, I can't totally switch off, I keep in contact with the lads who are still out there. Maybe it's loyalty, maybe it's guilt, maybe it's just habit.

And then there's Sarah. Things aren't right between us. There's a distance I can't quite bridge. I don't know if she's found someone else, I don't want to believe it, but she feels. , , , detached. She moans at me about crumbs on the counter or clothes left out after a shower, and I want to scream: *Are you serious?*

It's like I've become an intruder in my own home. She's got her routines, her friends, her world and I'm just a visitor passing through.

Kyle doesn't understand all of it, not really. One of the kids at school told him I was going to die in Iraq, and it rattled him. He doesn't ask me questions anymore. I think he knows, in his own way, that it's dangerous, but he pushes it down. Pretends it isn't real.

I booked a holiday for us, hoping it might help. A bit of sun, a change of scenery. We're by the pool, watching Kyle play and laugh in the water. I glance over at Sarah, and the thought just comes, *I don't know if we're going to make it.*

She has her own life, the animals, the horses, a whole separate world I'm not really part of anymore. And when I'm back, I don't fit into it. Gym sessions are the only real structure I have. The money's fine. That's not the problem.

The problem is harder to name. It's in my gut, this quiet emptiness. Like something's gone.

I don't know what it is.

I just know . . .I'm not whole.

Before heading back out to Iraq, I always spend quality time with my mum and my grandparents. Family means everything to me, and despite the job, I've managed to stay close to them. They never ask what exactly I do over there, and I don't volunteer any details either, it's an unspoken agreement we've developed over the years. There's really no sense in burdening them with the reality of my work. I've seen enough worry etched into their faces when I say goodbye at the door; they don't need the added stress of knowing specifics.

When I'm out on operations, I check in with them every couple of weeks on the sat phone. Those brief conversations, filled mostly with mundane chit-chat about home, weather, and what's happening in the garden, mean more than I can ever express. For a few moments, it helps ground me, reminds me there's a life away from the sand, heat, and constant danger.

I know that every morning without fail, they're switching on the TV, nervously watching the news reports from Iraq, just hoping and praying nothing too serious has kicked off overnight. It's a strange comfort for me, knowing that whatever they're seeing, it isn't the reality I face every day. If they don't witness the firefights, explosions, or the sheer chaos that has become my normal, then that's enough peace of mind for me.

Maybe one day, years from now, we'll sit down, and I'll share some of the stories with them, carefully edited, of course. But until then, this unspoken agreement between us holds firm. Their ignorance is my protection for them; it's the least I can do.

BACK IN: July 2007

Alright folks, it's been a while since I've had a chance to check in, things have been relatively steady here, or at least as steady as Baghdad ever gets. The daily incident count has dropped from a staggering 100-

plus a day down to somewhere around 50 or 60. This is made up of car bombs, IEDs, ambushes etc. Still dangerous, still unpredictable, but oddly enough, it feels almost manageable by comparison.

The Americans have ramped things up again, another 3,000 troops flown in to tighten the grip on the city. Everywhere you look now, these towering concrete T, walls are going up, cutting the place into sectors. It's like living inside a giant Lego city built by someone with a paranoia complex.

Inside camp, we're still getting hit. Mortars and rockets rain in like clockwork, doesn't matter what the news says. Only yesterday we took nineteen mortars in a single barrage. Absolute chaos. Bodies everywhere. One poor American girl was just walking between buildings when a round landed, took her head clean off. Just like that. Gone. Nothing about it made the headlines back home, of course. Just another day in Baghdad.

On a different note, something big might be brewing. Word just came down the wire that there's an opening for the second, in, command slot on General Scott's Personal Security Detail.

A lot of people ask the same question: *Why are civilian contractors protecting high-ranking military officers? Shouldn't the military be looking after their own?*

It's a fair question, on the surface. But here's the truth most people don't know: your average soldier, no matter how well-trained in combat, isn't trained in *close protection*. That's a completely different skill set.

We're not talking about kicking in doors or clearing compounds. Close protection is about precision, anticipation, and control. It's about reading a situation before anything happens, scanning a street corner and spotting a threat before it even materialises. You've got to be switched on 24/7, ready to extract your principal under fire, navigate IED-riddled roads, or get them out of a contact zone with no warning and no backup. It's not just muscle and rifles, it's planning, movement drills, low-profile ops, deception tactics. It's a mindset.

That's where companies like Aegis come in. They hold the contract for the protection of military brass, generals, commanders, diplomats. These are high-value individuals who operate outside the wire, in volatile environments where the usual rules don't apply. And they need people who specialise in keeping them alive.

The military knows this. That's why they outsource to guys like us. Most of us come from specialist units, Operators that specialise in close protection, operators with real-world experience in hostile environments. We've trained for this. We've lived it.

So next time someone asks, *'Why are civilians protecting military officers?'* – there's your answer. Because when it comes to high-level close protection in a war zone, it's not about the uniform. It's about who can get the job done.

So, this is not just any job, this is *General Scott* we're talking about. A two-star general and the top man in Joint Central Command for Iraq and Afghanistan. He doesn't just oversee operations, he *controls the entire budget* for both theatres. Every contract, every asset, every dollar. Nothing moves without his say, so. The man is a power broker at the very top, and anyone near him needs to be rock-solid, squared away, and razor-sharp.

He runs with a tight six-man PSD team, his very own shadow unit that moves when he moves, flies when he flies, eats when he eats. And now there's a vacancy for the second in command. That kind of role isn't advertised, it's *whispered*.

I've got an inside track, his current Team Leader, Hugh, or 'Big Shug' as I call him. He comes from the same close protection background as me, so we speak the same language. No ego, no fluff, just solid, professional know how. He's sharp, calm under pressure, polite, diplomatic but to the point. Doesn't waste words and doesn't need to.

We've worked together before and got on well, same mindset, same twisted sense of humour that gets you through the darker days out here. Had a proper chat with him today and I came away buzzing. He reckons I'd be a strong fit, said I've got what it takes to step up and run the show when he's on leave.

That's all the green light I needed.

And truth be told, this is the kind of gig I've been working toward since I set foot in country. The SET teams are great – plenty of action, plenty of responsibility – but this . . . this is different. This is high profile, front-line protection for one of the most powerful men in-theatre. You're not just another gun in a convoy, you *are the barrier* between life and death for a VIP who holds the keys to the whole region. It's the kind of role that opens doors. It commands respect. Guys who've done this job don't need to explain their CV, people just understand what type of bloke you are.

The prestige alone is massive. You're instantly in a different league, trusted at the highest level, Top secret clearance, briefed on classified routes, privy to meetings that shape the war. It's close protection in its purest form. High risk, high stakes, but if you're switched on and capable, it's exactly where you want to be.

This could be the move that changes everything. I'm going for it.

If I manage to impress them enough and get the position, I'll need to do a Team Leaders Cadre, a two-week hammering that's basically a compressed version of junior Brecon. Full-on intensive leadership and tactics course that's taught in the military before promotion.

This could be a career-defining move if I play it right. High risk, high reward, but then again, that's been the story of this whole damn place.

Let's see what happens.

June 2007 – Baghdad Set 1

Chris (Kid), Tom, and the guys from Set 1 were out today on a mission when they were hit badly. Like I mentioned before, the team is made up of international operators with a local guy as an interpreter. Evan, on Set 1, was an excellent lad, Western ways, gym bunny, and very capable of holding his own in a firefight. Chris was in the lead vehicle, near the slip road back toward the Green Zone, everything changed in an instant. An EFP array detonated without warning.

Chris told me he didn't hear it as much as he felt it, the violence of it. The truck rocked, and Tom started screaming in the back. That's when he realised, he'd been hit. His left thigh felt like it had been smashed by a hammer, and flames were licking at his arm and neck. The vehicle was on fire, but he didn't stop. He ignored the pain and stayed focused on what mattered: driving!

With the power dead, he coasted the truck at around 45mph, just steering and hoping to get the team out of the kill zone. Smoke filled the cab. He tried to open the windows, but they wouldn't budge more than a crack. He hit the door lock, tried the handle, nothing. The sulphur stench of the blast hung thick in the air.

He stayed calm. Told himself to focus, to drive through it. But the flames were growing, and the smoke was turning black and suffocating. He couldn't see. Couldn't breathe. The moment he started to think about stopping, Tom screamed from the back, 'Pull over!'

Chris tried the brakes, but they barely responded – likely the booster was gone. So, he did what only instinct and experience can teach, he threw the truck into a high concrete curb to slow down. Grinding metal and sparks. It slowed just enough. He straightened the truck and brought it to a full stop.

That's when things got worse.

They both scrambled for the doors. Nothing opened. Smoke was building rapidly, like a curtain had been pulled over their faces. Chris said later it was like breathing in but getting nothing. Suffocating while fully conscious. He thought, *this is it.*

Then he heard a voice in his head, calm, firm: 'If you don't open that door, everyone's going to die.'

He forced himself to slow down, like swimming underwater, and started feeling around. Couldn't see a thing, but somehow managed to get the door open with one last push.

He tumbled out and sucked in air. But before he could even get his bearings, he heard Tom inside, still trapped. Chris went straight back in.

Calling out, he told Tom to move toward him. He reached through the smoke and felt his gear. Started pulling. But the centre console and Codan radio blocked him. He tried again, elbows in tight, straining for leverage. The heat was burning his face. Still, he kept going.

Eventually, he had to step out or collapse. Panic set in, he didn't know how to get Tom the rest of the way out.

That's when one of the other lads appeared.

Chris was pulled back from the fire. Others were shouting and pulling too, but he wasn't done. He went to Evan's door and got it open, but there was no response inside. Someone dragged me away, he said, and he hit the deck outside, gasping, unable to move.

He looked back and saw the other lads diving into the burning truck. Moments later, they emerged, dragging Tom out. They started working on Tom's body armour. Chris tried to speak, to tell them how to release it, but he couldn't. Just opened his mouth, pointed.

Then gunfire erupted. Wilson from the team was returning fire toward the six. It wasn't just traffic, it was incoming.

At this point, Chris forced himself up and limped to the rear vehicle. Rick, who was also on the team, pointed an M4 at him in the chaos, but Smith shouted and broke the moment. Together, they lifted Tom and carried him to the vehicle. Chris climbed in first, struggling with his leg. Smith shoved Tom's legs in like a backwards somersault and slammed the door.

Chris collapsed into the footwell, gasping, helmet off, just trying to breathe. 'It'll pass,' he told himself.

Then he heard Tom's voice: 'Kid . . . where's Kid?'

Chris rasped, 'Tom, I'm here. I'm okay.'

Smith asked about Evan. Al shook his head. Smith muttered something under his breath. They knew he was gone.

The convoy tore through Checkpoint 12 at the entrance to the Green Zone. Smith drove like a lunatic, bouncing over speed bumps, pushing through counterflow. A rear panel nearly cracked Chris across the skull. He caught Wilson's eye, they both gave each other a faint, mad little smile. Still alive.

Wilson tried to apply a tourniquet to Chris's leg. Chris waved him off. Said it'd hurt too much. Wilson snapped, 'Look at your leg!'

Chris looked down. Blood everywhere. Down his inner thigh into his boot. 'I don't think it's mine,' he barked.

They reached the CSH (Combat Support Hospital). Chris insisted, 'Get Tom out first.' Then the pain came in waves. They stripped his kit and wheeled him in. One of the clients pushed his gurney to the trauma bay.

Inside, medics worked fast. IV in before he could speak. But they forgot to open the oxygen valve. He kept saying he couldn't breathe. Eventually, someone noticed and flipped it on.

Then came the blindness. Chris shouted, 'Hey, I can't see!' Stars everywhere. Shock or adrenaline, it passed. But it rattled him.

Smith and the lads came in and said, 'You did a good job, man.'

'That was some good driving, kid.'

Chris asked, '. . . Evan?'

Smith just said again, 'You did a good job.'

That's when he knew.

The Bubble

We live in Baghdad's Green Zone, for you that are not aware, let me explain . . .

A four-square-mile fortress of concrete T-Walls with manned checkpoints at every entrance. It's located in the heart of a city. Outside the wire, Baghdad burned. Inside, it was something else entirely. Safe, they said. Secure. But anyone who spends time here knows better. The Green Zone isn't safe; it is just *safer*.

I remember the first time I passed through Checkpoint 12, the main gate. Triple-layered security, ID checks, dogs sniffing every vehicle for explosives. Iraqi guards watched us from behind sandbagged towers, while US MPs eyeballed everyone like they expected trouble, because they did, this was the entrance to everything, and car bombs hit it almost once a week. There is a long line of Iraqi locals who work in here lined up first thing in the morning waiting to be searched and passes given. Once you were inside though, it feels like stepping through a portal. From chaos to control. From war torn streets to . . . Green Beans coffee houses and salad bars. We have McDonalds, Pizza Hut, Subway and locals that were security cleared even have their own market stalls selling hooky DVDs.

The US carved this place out of Saddam Hussein's old stomping grounds, his palaces, his ministries, his legacy. Now it was a Coalition stronghold, a strange fusion of Western order and crumbling Ba'athist grandeur. The Republican Palace has become the US Embassy compound. Marble floors and grand paintings on the wall. Chandeliers hang above racks of M4 rifles. Saddam's old toilets are used by American generals and contractors. If he could've seen it, he would have choked on his cigar.

We live in long rows of two-storey apartments, probably built as holiday chalets years ago, from the look of them. Solid brick construction, so they offer decent protection against incoming mortars. Each one has its own en suite, air-conditioned, with just enough space for a bed, a TV, and a small clothing cupboard. Basic, but it does the job. You still go to sleep at night with your weapons close to hand and your boots by the door, just in case the sirens go off. And they do most nights.

'Incoming, incoming, incoming!' The voice of the alarm still makes my stomach tighten. Mortars and rockets, frequent visitors. You never get used to that sound. When you first come into country, you dive for cover and go to the mobile shelter when the rockets come into camp, now after a few years, I just pull my duvet over my head and wait and see what happens. You become so desensitised, even when one hits meters away. It's a bad mindset I suppose but I think, if my time is up, it's up.

We have lost vehicles, buildings, and unfortunately there have been multiple casualties from the barrage of incoming. Sometimes, you hear the whistle as it flies past you then you see the explosion, all you say is, fuck me, that was close!

But the weirdest part? Between the blasts and blackouts, life inside the Green Zone is almost . . . normal. *Too normal.*

There are gyms, big ones. Bench presses, squat racks, treadmills. You can find meatheads yelling over Metallica in one corner, while a group of Marines do curls and argued about college football. Some guy's train like their lives depended on it. In a way, they did. Physical strength was currency out here, it keeps you sane, keeps you sharp.

Then there are the DFACs. Massive dining facilities with air-conditioning and rows of food counters. You can get steak one night, tacos the next. Ice cream flows like a river, and you see guys piling plates like they hadn't eaten in weeks. I remember walking past a guy once with pizza, a cheeseburger, and a lobster tail on the same tray. War makes you greedy in strange ways.

On base, you can find a PX loaded with American junk food, DVDs, bootleg CDs and knockoff Oakley's. Contractors, soldiers, diplomats, everyone mills around in a surreal blend of tactical vests, uniforms and baseball caps. It looked like a Walmart in a war zone. Some days you'd see a guy sipping a caramel frappuccino from the Green Bean coffee stand while a Blackhawk buzzed low overhead. The disconnect was dizzying.

What do we do in the evening when we're not out on missions? well believe it or not, the teams usually get together, play pool and have a laugh. The PX have Xboxes for sale, we bought one with a projector and stream it onto the side of a building within the complex and play Call of duty, it's good to let off steam and of course, we take the piss out of each other most of the time too. We have internet in our bunks here with a connection to home, Skype is great unless it's from one of the lads, usually Mark, you open the video link and he's windmilling his knob at you, creature!

The Americans run the show, but there are Brits, Aussies, contractors from every walk of life, SAS lads, Paras, Marines, former Foreign Legion. We all have our own little groups tucked into different corners. Some live near Camp Prosperity or Union III, others inside embassy compounds with tighter security and better perks. A couple of times I've seen a few Hummers rolling out with the Punisher symbol painted on the front, not sure who it is though.

Security is everything. Movement outside the Green Zone requires armoured convoys and QRF backup. Inside, you still wear your sidearm. Paranoia doesn't sleep. Even at the pool, yes, there is a swimming pool, Saddam's old one, it's surrounded by blast walls and a posted guard. You can float on your back and watch Apaches fly overhead. A war within earshot.

The Green Zone isn't home, It's a pressure cooker. A bubble filled with overstretched nerves, half, truths, and false comfort. You can eat three hot meals a day and still feel empty. You can pump iron and still feel powerless. You can wear body armour and still feel naked.

Some never leave the wire. They do their tour entirely inside this concrete shell and go home thinking they had seen war. But those of us who are out most days rolling into the Red Zone on ops, we knew the truth.

The Green Zone is never real.

It just helps you forget, for a little while, while everything around you is on fire.

Monday 20 August 2007

Interviews today for the new job, there are eight of us in the running. Good mix of lads, a few with serious combat experience. Some of them probably have seen more combat than me, at least in uniform. Hard to say. What stands out, though, was how quickly the cracks show when it comes to actually talking.

Don't get me wrong, they're great blokes. Soldiers. Trained to follow orders, fight through contact, get the job done. But put them in a room with high-ranking brass, and it's like they shrink. Mumbling, stumbling over words, or trying too hard to impress. That whole 'Yes Sir, No Sir' routine, but without the polish.

That's where I think I've got the edge. My background's not all green kit and guns blazing, I came from the civilian close protection world. Spent years dealing with diplomats, celebrities and corporate heads. People who expect you to vanish into the background until something goes wrong and then fix it without drama. That job's not just about soldiering. It's about presence, how you carry yourself, how you read a room and put clients at ease without saying much.

In the interview, I didn't waffle. Just told them what I've done, what I've seen. Spoke straight. I know how to do the job, and more importantly, I know how to behave in front of the people we're supposed to protect. It's not just about guarding bodies, it's about guarding reputations, appearances and keeping control.

We'll see what happens. I reckon I think it went well, but who knows what box they're looking to tick. Either way, I was myself, no act, no fluff, just laid it out. If they want real, world experience and someone who knows both sides of the fence, military and civilian, then hopefully they can see that in me.

I head back to my bunk, downed a bottle of Gatorade and wait . . . I wonder when I will hear anything? I know there are a few *American* lads in for it and maybe because it's an *American* general, they'll get the job.

21 August 2007

Up at 0700hrs to get scoff from the DFAC. The team has some down time today so, Breakfast, Gym coffee and chill for a change. I was just about to jump in the shower when my phone rings . . . It's the boss, 'Scott, you need to pack up your room, you got the job, and I need you to move over to the General's compound. There is a connex ready to move into and you'll be doing a TL Cadre starting tomorrow.' **YES!!**

Chapter 12

The General's Team

Being on the General's team is such a big deal for me. It means no more running the gauntlet through Baghdad waiting for the next EFP to rip through me or the next round bouncing off the wagon. No more endless road moves, checkpoints, or holding your breath at every junction. The days of getting shot at, blown up, or returning fire while ambushed, for now at least, are behind me.

Most of our movements are by air now, with just the occasional road move with a dedicated SET team. We have Blackhawks or fixed-wing private US military aircraft at our disposal. The General even has access to his own jet, a Gucci piece of kit like you see in the movies. It feels like flying on a mini-Air Force One. We're moving across the Middle East like ghosts, in and out of high, security zones, Quatar, Afghanistan, Dubai no drama.

There's a bit of glamour to it, I won't lie. The prestige that comes with this job is next level. As a bodyguard, this is about as high up the ladder as you can get. Trusted, respected, and right at the heart of it all , but in a completely different way.

I'm proud to be on this team. After everything I've seen, everything I've done, this feels like something to hold onto.

Here is my New Boss…

MAJOR GENERAL DARRYL A. SCOTT
Maj. Gen. Darryl A. Scott is Deputy Commander, Task Force to Support Business and Stability Operations in Iraq, Office of the Deputy

Under Secretary of Defence (Business Transformation), and Deputy Director, Defence Business Transformation Agency, the Pentagon, Washington, D.C.

A native of Washington, D.C., General Scott entered the Air Force after graduating from the US Air Force Academy in June 1974. After initial assignments in computer operations, he transitioned to the contracting career field. He has subsequently served as a principal contracting officer for space, missile, aircraft, and command, control, communications, computers, intelligence, surveillance and reconnaissance systems. He commanded three times; served as Vice Commander, Warner Robins Air Logistics Center, Robins Air Force Base, Ga.; and as Director, Defence Contract Management Agency, Alexandria, Va. He has served staff tours at both major command and Air Staff levels.

I have met the current team, a cracking bunch of lads . .

There's six of us on the General's team.

Matt's a good mate; we've worked together previously on the SET teams. He's ex-Logistics Corps and served as a CP driver for a three-star UK General here while still in the military, so he knows the drills.

He's been on the team for about 6 months. A big lad at 6ft 2, muscular, shaved head. Looks like he could snap your neck but actually one of the nicest blokes you will meet. Easy to talk to, no ego. Just a really nice big guy. His wife works out here in the office too, a real family affair

Hugh's the team leader or 'Shuggy' as I call him. About 5ft 10, A big lad, shaved head and a goatee. knows his stuff too. Loads of experience in the civilian CP world. We both agree on how things should be run, which makes the job nice and fluid. No power trips, just mutual respect.

Then there's Henk and Chris, the two South Africans. Middle-aged and inseparable, when off duty you'll always see them with a smoke hanging from their mouths and a coffee. They've been in the game forever. Sure, they're a bit rough around the edges and definitely won't be winning any fitness contests, but they've spent years in-country and know the place inside out. Solid operators. The other teams might take the piss behind their backs, but I've got a lot of time for them.

And then there's young Chris. He's 25, did a few years in the US Marines, keeps himself to himself, quiet, hard to read. Spends most of his time behind the wheel. Didn't say much at first, getting more than two words out of him was like pulling teeth. But I've made the effort to get to know him.

And I'm glad I did.

I've spent a bit of time working alongside him recently, and truth is, he's a good lad. Got the right mindset. We're on the same page when it comes to how the job should be done. His professionalism is spot on. Whether it's driving or on the ground with the client, he's switched on and does not miss a beat. He's still young, still learning, but he has got something about him, and he likes his fitness routine too.

I've done the Cadre, moved into my new bunk across from the general and I'm about to meet him . . .

My New Boss

I headed over to the General's office to introduce myself and have a quick chat. Honestly, I was impressed straight away. He is softly spoken, clearly switched on, and has this quiet confidence about him, an aura that everyone notices immediately.

He welcomed me warmly, asked me to take a seat, and then started asking about me, asked about family and background and always looked interested. It felt more like I was being brought into a family unit rather than joining a rigid military hierarchy. After a brief chat it was back to business, calling him Sir and keeping protocol again.

General Scott works out of a secure office inside a larger, locked-down office area here on camp, where he does his thing supported by a full team.

His aide-de-camp, Commander Grow, goes everywhere with him, quietly efficient and always respectful. Then there's his Chief of Staff, a larger-than-life Captain who's funny, outgoing, and has eyes on absolutely everything happening here. He keeps the General clued up on certain parts of the project here.

There's the command Sgt Major Hernandez or 'Lupe'. He could be as gentle as a grandfather or the scariest man on earth, depending on the situation. I never heard him raise his voice though. A real cool character always smiling and walks with an air of confidence. Nothing seems to faze him.

The office has a whole bunch of other military personnel working for him, Vicky, Sgt. Baker, Troy, Caeser, and us. There's always two of us stationed right across from the General. He's never alone, not even when he nips off for a toilet break!

Commander Grow gives us the Boss's movements a few days in advance and a week if we are going out of country. We organise all the transport with Aegis including air cover, there's a lot of detail goes into planning movements with the boss which keeps us busy.

General Scott likes to go for a 3k run every morning around the camp. So, as you guess a couple of us have to go running with him, Chris and Matt usually volunteer as they like their cardio.

After his run and a shower, we head over to his bunk where we meet commander Grow. As the Boss opens his door, the commander is stood at attention and they both exchange salutes while we are in position with the door open, engine running and driver in place, he always greets us with a smile, a nod and a 'good morning gentlemen' before we take him to the embassy for breakfast then his morning meetings.

In the embassy we have brilliant scoff, top quality, you can get anything here, I usually get far too much as it's so tempting to overeat. We move as soon as he does and go about our day one of us only an arm's length away, it's a well-oiled machine, we are always in comms via radios with each other and have direct comms with Aegis HQ.

I saw something today that properly pissed me off. We were doing our usual weekly visit to the military hospital with the General. It's normally just routine, shake a few hands, check on the wounded lads, try to boost morale. But today . . . today was different.

Out the corner of my eye, I noticed something that didn't belong, a tiny baby. Lying there in an American military hospital bed. A baby? In a place like this? I couldn't get my head around it. I asked one of the doctors what had happened.

He walked me over, and there she was. A little girl, maybe five months old. Dried blood still on her face, tubes everywhere, her chest rising and falling like a bird struggling to breathe. Then he told me, she'd been shot.

Shot. Who the fuck shoots a baby?

Turns out her family were being threatened by an Al-Qaeda cell in their village. The usual intimidation, give up your home to us or else. Her dad refused to leave, brave man. But they came anyway.

They broke in and shot his wife dead while she was holding the baby, right there. No hesitation. One round tore through the baby's tiny chest and shoulder. The mother died on the spot, but the baby survived, barely.

I stood there and gently held her little hand. Just five months old and already living through hell. What a way to start a life. Scarred in every sense. I thought I'd seen the worst this place could throw at us. But this . . . this took the fucking biscuit. Al-Qaeda are just total scum; there is no room on this earth for these people.

Every Friday evening, we fly over to Camp Victory within Baghdad International Airport. It's where all the top military brass are based. They took over all of Saddam's palaces over there and turned them into very posh headquarters.

We go there to meet General David Petraeus who was appointed by George Bush to be the commander-in-chief of Central Command here. When I say we go to meet him, the General has dinner with him while we sit in the kitchen with the grunts and shoot the shit.

We fly over there in three Blackhawk helicopter formation and back when it's black as night. The first time flying over Baghdad at night always catches you out. The pilots fly with night vision and there's no lights in the chopper, then you come to an area before coming to land where the pilots let of a multitude of flares just in case there's a threat, and you shit yourself. It's funny when you see blokes for the first time, Eyes wide open like a deer caught in headlights.

Instead of just two of the CP team going to a function, the whole team got asked to tag along with General Scott to one at the US Embassy tonight. We knew there was an awards ceremony on for the brass, so we figured it was just business as usual. Stand at the back, stay switched on, look the part.

Halfway through, the General gets up to speak. He thanks his staff, nothing out the ordinary, then calls them forward to receive his personal 'Coin of Excellence'. These things aren't just tokens, expertly crafted gold coins, embossed with his name, rank, and the US flag. He only gives them out in rare, significant moments. It's the closest thing to a personal medal you can get from him.

We watched the officers and captains go up, one by one, collect theirs, shake his hand. Thought that was it.

Then he called us, 'Swordfish 6, can you come up please . . .'
Didn't expect that. Not one bit.

He stood there and said he wanted to thank his Close Protection team with the same honour. Said we'd earned it. Handed each of us his coin, looked us in the eye, hugged us, and said, *'I'd trust my life anywhere with you.'*

Wow, what a genuine gesture. We were honoured, truly. Didn't see it coming, and it meant the world. That coin's not just a piece of metal, it's a reminder that sometimes, the work gets noticed.

That's made my year.

I've been on the General's team for quite some time now and although it's a great gig, I'm starting to get itchy feet. I've been in and out of war zones for seven years almost and I think I need a change. I am making a lot of money but I'm not getting the chance to enjoy it. Yeah, I make sure the family don't want for anything, but as I'm here for nine months out of the year I don't have much of a life, and then I think: If I die over here, what have I accomplished?

Kyle is growing up quick and I am missing out on a lot of his life. I see him and Sarah are enjoying the money, going on holidays together, buying more horses and going about their life without me in it. Am I just a bank to them?

What if I go home, what will I do? Can I handle civvy life? Am I willing to try? What about the future? I wish someone or something would take these decisions out of my hands . . .

The General has told us this morning that his time is up here and he's finally going home soon. He was originally only meant to be for 12 months, which was 2 years ago! Poor man must be threaders.

The team will be sad to see him go to be honest; there is one thing I have always been asked about being a bodyguard . . . 'Would you take a bullet for your client?' As I sit here now, I can honestly say 'YES' and that's unusual as clients go, he's been the best one yet.

Not only is the General going, but all his immediate staff too, Commander Grow, his Aide will be replaced, his PA etc. Maybe this is the change I have been looking for?

His replacement will be here in a couple of weeks and the only thing I've heard it's a woman. I don't know who or what she will be like, but fingers crossed.

There will be a big ceremony here in a few weeks for the handover with all the heads invited, General Petraeus is coming along with Iraqi prime minister. If anyone is going to take any of them out, this would be the time.

You wouldn't believe the planning involved in such a display, we're working constantly getting this organised.

The Rear Admiral

We have been told about our new boss, she will be flying in and shadowing the general for short time. She is a Rear Admiral of the US Navy, well suited for the role I'm hearing.

Kathleen M. Dussault graduated from the University of Virginia with a Bachelor of Arts in American Government, received her commission from Officer Candidate School in Newport, R.I., in November 1979, and graduated from Navy Supply Corps School in May 1980.

Dussault has served on USS *Point Loma* (AGDS 2) in the Pacific Area Launch Support Ship for the Trident missile program as supply officer; USS *Concord* (AFS 5) as the assistant supply officer during Operations Desert Shield and Desert Storm, and as supply officer aboard USS Seattle (AOE 3) where she served as afloat logistics coordinator while deployed to the US 5th Fleet area of operation.

Her decorations include a Defence Superior Service Medal, Legion of Merit with two gold stars, Bronze Star, Navy Meritorious Service Medal with two gold stars, Joint Service Commendation Medal, Navy and Marine Corps Commendation Medal, Navy and Marine Corps Achievement Medal with gold star, and various unit citations, campaign medals and service medals.

Goodbye to the General

We were escorting General Scott to the airstrip for his flight out of this long tour. He'd been quiet the whole drive, just staring out the window like he was replaying everything in his head.

When we got to the jet, he walked up the steps slowly, then stopped. Turned around. His eyes locked onto ours.

'Gentlemen,' he said, voice shaking, 'I'd go anywhere with you. You kept me alive . . . my wife and kids' – his voice cracked –' they thank you too.'

You could see the emotion building in him. He wasn't just saying it, he meant it. You could feel the weight behind his words. His eyes started welling up, but he held it together just enough.

He stepped down from the stairs, came over, and hugged us both like a man who knew what it meant to owe his life to someone. Then he stood back, straightened his uniform, gave us a slow, deliberate salute.

'God bless you. I'll never forget you.'

Then he turned and boarded.

We stood there watching the jet roll down the tarmac. That moment . . . Reality hit us. Because in that instant, we knew, we weren't just bodyguards. We were the reason he was going home.

The handover's done. Rear Admiral's in the hot seat now, and we're back to work as normal with a new Principal.

It's a different vibe altogether with the new boss. She's got a calm, pleasant way about her, easy to talk to, very sharp minded. But I'll admit, the knitting on the C-130 threw me. There we were, sat opposite each other mid-flight, coming back from Afghanistan, pitch black in the netted fuselage with a bunch of US grunts, noise like thunder, and she's there calmly knitting a scarf or something. We laughed about it. Still, whatever keeps your head straight in this place, fair play to her.

We're bouncing all over the map now, she's got a taste for every dusty corner: Iraq, Afghanistan, Qatar, Dubai. One minute we're stepping off a private jet, the next we're rattling around in a Blackhawk. It's non-stop movement, always somewhere to be. Not much real action though, if I'm honest, but that's alright. I'm not chasing firefights anymore.

Compared to other gigs, this one's pretty tame. That said, we're still getting our fair share of mortars and rockets still landing in camp daily. Every Sunday we go to a church service run by the US military. Last Sunday the mortars started incoming while Mat and I were just outside in the truck. one landed so close it nearly turned the whole place into a memorial, and there's me, running to the main door. Booted it nearly off the hinges, running into the church like a madman, looking for her, everyone was on the floor and the admiral's colleague Sgt Baker is pointing . . . 'She's here'. A quick grab and into the truck and back to the office. That's about as much excitement I get now. I should be grateful, I know, I'm not being blown up and shot at every day, I should thank my lucky stars.

Chapter 13

The Accident

I got a call this morning, Sarah's been thrown from one of our horses. Crushed the base of her spine. They are saying it's bad . . . major surgery, and even then, there's a chance she might never walk again. Fuck. I need to get home. This isn't just a knock or a fracture, this could be life-changing.

Remember I didn't know what my next move was, and I asked the universe if it would be taken out my hands, well I guess this is it . . .

I spoke to the bosses, they said, yeah, go home, do what you need to do, then call us, your position will still be here when you return.

I am thinking about Kyle, he must be in a right state, who's going to look after him till I'm home?

It took me 16 hours to get back home, and I finally get to the hospital. Sarah is in a bad way, but she still finds time to moan at me for taking so long getting there, I can't win.

We chat about the operation, what the prognosis is and the recovery time. She tells me to go and get Kyle; he's at a neighbour's house.

I go pick up Kyle and try to tell him things will be fine, I'm home, I'm going nowhere, and mum will be just fine. He has this worried look and is asking me when can we go see mum? I told him later, after we get him home and settled. We sat watching telly while I ordered dinner and got some shopping in. He's 11 years old now, so grown up for his age and such a good polite boy. I'm really proud of him. He's handling this really well.

Sarah called, she's out of surgery, operation went well but although, she will be able to walk again, the nerves are damaged so there will be no real feeling from the waist down. Shit, how is this going to work? What about my job, our future, taking care of Kyle?

It has been a few months since the accident. Sarah's recovering, aye, but let's be honest, it's me doing everything. I know in sickness and in health and all that, but Jesus, a bit of appreciation wouldn't go amiss. Feels like I'm not her husband anymore, just her carer. Taxi driver. Cleaner. And with Kyle, I'm basically a single parent as well – school runs, dinners, washing and ironing his clothes, everything.

I keep telling myself, she'll get better soon. But truth is, I'm on my knees here. I don't know how much more I've got in the tank. This isn't living – it's just surviving, and not the kind I'm used to. Sarah is a strong woman, stubborn and self-sufficient, she hates when I ask if I can physically help her, she just says no and pushes me away. So, my focus is on keeping Kyle happy.

Life on deployment is simpler. Out there, my washing gets done and delivered, my meals are sorted, my day is mapped out precisely. All I have to worry about is making sure my boss and my team get home alive, dodging mortars and staying sharp. That's straight forward, almost easy, compared to the relentless pressure I'm under right now.

My mental state is slowly deteriorating, what's happening to me? I just don't feel right. I can't leave the house, I can't be with people, I'm constantly on edge, and the dreams! The dreams are haunting me. I still dress as if I'm back out there, I can't shake this. Sarah is recovering and walking now and helping out when she can, but we are not a couple anymore, we hardly speak, sleep in separate rooms, What the fuck has happened?

I wanted a change from the sandpit, but this is not what I expected. I think it's time for me to go back to my *real* life again.

We all had a chat today and I said ' I think it's time for me to return to work'. It's been three months and Sarah is back, slowly helping with the horses, Kyle at school and going through the emotions of an 11-year-old ready to start high school. Time for me to go. She didn't really say much to be honest, happy for me to go I guess, I'm just a lodger in my own home anyway. Kyle understood that I had to make money to pay the bills and keep them in the lifestyle they have come to expect now.

I'm calling work tomorrow to get my flights booked.

Just got off the phone to HQ in Iraq. Called HR, spoke to Milly, I let her know I was ready to redeploy, bags packed, head in the game, good to go. Then she drops a fucking grenade on me.

'I'm really sorry, Scott. Your contract's been terminated. We won't be asking you back.'

Are you joking? Are you serious? My position was supposed to be secure, open door, any time. So, what the fuck's happened now?

She says they found a bag of 5.56 rounds under my bunk. Unregistered ammo. Contract breach.

Absolute bollocks. No way. That bunk was spotless, I sanitised the place top to bottom, same as I always do. Those rounds were not mine! Never were. Somebody's stitched me up good and proper.

All she gives me is a half-hearted sorry, like it's nothing. Sorry? That's it? I've been loyal, dependable, never kicked up a fuss, never bitched or moaned, always delivered, always went above and beyond. This stinks, and there's more to it. I know there is.

I started making calls. Spoke to a mate still out there. He saw one of the SET lads going into my bunk with a bag just after I left, an ex-team mate too! He didn't really think of it at the time, he said, that makes sense . . . he was eyeing up my role for weeks. Turns out he wanted it bad. Real bad. That sneaky little fuck planted the rounds. Framed me.

And guess what? Apparently, he's been shagging Milly, the HR witch herself. The one who signs off on deployments. How fucking convenient, eh? Always someone ready to stick a blade in your back in this line of work. Jealousy's a cancer out there. Eats away at everything. I'd seen it before. Same pattern, different uniform.

When I joined Aegis, an ex-teammate from my old unit decided I was doing too well for his liking. Instead of cracking on, he went round the circuit posting a load of shite, telling anyone who'd listen that I was a coward, that I made up my stories, that I was all mouth and no substance. funny enough, he didn't use his real name on the emails either.

The blokes who actually knew me knew exactly what it was. Jealous nonsense. Sour grapes from someone who couldn't stand seeing another man get ahead. Their opinions were the only ones that mattered.

But that's the reality of this game. There's always someone watching, always someone waiting for a chance to pull you down rather than put the work in themselves. Jealousy's a terrible curse in this world, quiet, poisonous, and usually wielded by the people closest to you.

I have told Sarah what happened. She didn't take it well. Not because of the setup, not because I'd been stabbed in the back. No, 'What's going to happen when the money dries up?' she asks. Yeah, we've got enough in the bank to coast for a year or two, but still . . . what now?

Do I stay here? Try and build something? Find a job that doesn't eat away at my soul? Or do I find another company and start again?

Chapter 14

Behind the Mask

February 2010

I'm in a bad place right now. Sleep is impossible, my mind just won't switch off, it keeps replaying the same shit, the same memories from Iraq, over and over. One minute I'm watching TV, the next I'm right back there, feeling the heat, smelling the dry dust, hearing the chaos. How can it feel so real when I'm just sitting here in my own living room, supposed to be safe?

Sarah and I hardly talk anymore; she's usually in bed by 8pm, even before that, she lies on the sofa drugged up on pain killers, on her phone texting and playing games in silence. Kyle spends his time shut away in his room on his Xbox and listening to music, then there's me, wide awake, sat staring blankly at the TV

I've started drinking lately. I never used to touch alcohol at home, never felt the need, but now it seems to be the only thing that even slightly quietens my mind and blurs the images.

Tomorrow, I plan on getting out of the house, this is ridiculous. I need to sort myself out.

0700hrs

I'm awake. Didn't sleep well. Today, I'm forcing myself out the door. Gym's the target, lift some iron, smash the routine, and see what comes next.

The house is quiet. Kyle's sorting his school stuff, headphones on, Sarah's heading out early to the livery yard, brushing down the horses as she always does now. I won't see either of them until late afternoon, I might even get an hour with them before bed.

After the gym I needed to go get shopping. halfway through the supermarket run, my trolley's full but so am I, with tension that won't let up. People all bustling about, I'm sure I can hear everyone thinking, the noise is deafening the feeling of overwhelming anxiety Then just out of the blue this fat prick shoves me, just to step in front for a can of fucking beans!

'Oi, what the fuck, pal?'

He doesn't blink. 'What?' he snaps back, all arrogance. He's daring me.

I'm inches from him now, blood boiling. 'You fat fucker. Want to step outside for a fucking chat, you ignorant prick?'

I'm just full of rage. He shakes his head and walks away 'You're off your head, mate.'

Am I? Off my head, maybe he's right. He doesn't know the last seven years of my life. Does he get the sleepless nights? The flashbacks that hit me in the middle of the night or in a supermarket aisle. That smell of dust, the echo of gunshots? The rage of being helpless when blokes died?

In my head, I'm tearing at his face, beating him until there's nothing left. The darkness is that close. Fuck . . . maybe I am off my head. Maybe I should leave before I see him again and loose it. I just left my trolley and left, *just get to the car*, I'm thinking.

I'm sat there gripping the steering wheel, knuckles white, breathing ragged, I forced myself to calm down. I couldn't go back home, not just yet, I need to just wait here till the mist clears.

People I know are saying things like 'You must be glad to be home' or 'it must be good to get back to normal life'.

Normal?

They don't get it. How do you explain to someone that you still scan the roads for bombs while driving, you park your car facing out for a clean exit, scan the rooftops when you're in the city because habits don't die, they just stay welded in your nervous system like shrapnel in bone. You can't explain it, so I don't try . . .

I just laugh at their jokes, sit through small talk, nod my head when someone moans about getting stuck in traffic or their poxy internet speed is shite. What do I care?

The day-to-day is fucking draining. It's chewing me up, bit by bit. Sarah's still in pain even now, 24hrs a day, after her surgery, but when I ask if she's alright, if there's anything I can do, she just brushes it off. 'No, I'm fine.' Same answer every time. It's got to the stage I don't even bother asking now. What's the point? Just once, if she turned to me and said, 'Yeah, a hug would help', that would be something. But there's nothing. No warmth, no connection. I'm here, but I feel invisible. And honestly? I'm starting to wonder what my purpose is.

She has mentioned she thinks there's something wrong with me, 'You need to talk to someone,' she says. *Well, You're not helping*, I'm thinking, I want to scream but who the fuck do I talk to? Some strangers in a cardigan with a clipboard? What are they going to do, erase everything I've seen? Everything I've done? I don't think anyone can help me. I feel like I'm slipping, and no one's there to grab me. Certainly not Sarah, fuck she can hardly help herself never mind me. This is just me now. Damaged goods. I know it's PTSD. I'm not stupid. And I know I'm not alone, some of the lads I worked with, are back home feeling the same. Lost. Numb. It's like we all got shipped back in pieces, expected to just slot back into normal life. But I can't. I don't know how.

I finally face up to things and go see the doctor. I tell him everything and I can see the look of concern on his face. He gives me a prescription for Diazepam, sleeping pills and anti-depressants. He then sends a referral for me to see a shrink. I can't tell anyone, too embarrassed. *What the fuck is going on*, he looks at me and says it out loud. 'It's PTSD'. It's official now.

May 2010

I've been on the pills a few weeks now, waiting for the referral, but I'm just numb, lost in the fog. I'm sleeping a lot, can't stay awake, can't stay present. It's making things worse at home, Sarah barely looks at me, and Kyle, poor lad, just watches me like I'm some ghost in the corner. I've shut myself off completely. I don't go out. I don't talk. I can't face people anymore. I can't even face myself.

The flashbacks still punch through the meds, vivid, brutal, unforgiving. I'm back in that sandpit in seconds . . . the blood, the gunfire, the death, the heat of it all. It's too much. None of this is living anymore, it's just punishment. And I'm tired of being punished.

So, I've made a decision.

I'm going to end this suffering for everyone.

I've thought it through. Not out of drama or spite, but because I genuinely believe the world would be better off without me in it. I'm no good to Sarah. I'm failing Kyle. I'm dead weight dragging everyone down.

Maybe when I get to heaven, if I'm allowed through those gates, God will see past the things I've done. Maybe he'll understand why. Maybe I'll get another chance. And if there's such a thing as reincarnation, let me come back a better man next time. One who gets it right.

Because this version of me . . . this broken, bitter, hollow thing? He's done.

0900hrs

Everyone's out. The house is quiet. Kyle's at school, Sarah's up at the horses. No interruptions. No distractions. Just me and the end of this.

I've brought in the old photos, Kyle when he was wee, his smile so pure it hurts to look at. Sarah, back when things were good . . . when we still laughed, when there was still hope. I've laid them out on the bed beside me, like a final goodbye. A reminder of what I once had. What I've fucked up. What I've lost.

My grandparents are gone, they were my rock. And now, I've even pushed my own mum away. No phone calls. No support. Just silence. I've got no one left. I've backed myself into this dark corner and I can't find a way out.

The pills are here lined up neat. Sleeping tablets and Diazepam. My escape plan.

I can't keep hurting them. I can't keep waking up like this, drowning in guilt, in flashbacks, in this never, ending ache. I'm a burden. A fucking ghost in their house, They don't deserve this version of me.

I'm sorry . . . forgive me.

I take the pills, one, by one, by one. I stop counting after twenty. That's got to be enough, surely? I'm lying there, waiting, thinking. . . . this is it. I can feel the weight pulling me under, everything's slowing down. It's not painful, just heavy. Like my body's sinking into the mattress. My eyes are burning, and before I drift off, a single tear runs down my cheek. Not from fear . . . not even regret. Just pure, hopeless sadness.

Everything's white. There's this blinding light above me, getting brighter and brighter, I've finally done it.

But then I feel a hand on mine. Warm. Familiar. Sarah.

Fuck.

I'm in a hospital. I know it now. That sterile smell, the beeping machines, the weight in my chest. I don't want to open my eyes. I'm still out of it, but I know exactly where I am – and I've never felt more humiliated in my life.

It didn't work.

I'm still here.

And now I've got to face this.

I can hear Sarah's voice, quietly as she talks to a doctor at the side of the room. I roll my head away and cover my face with my arm, wishing the bed would just swallow me whole.

'What was that all about,' she says quietly, stepping closer. 'You know I had to perform CPR on you?' Jesus Christ.

I can't even look at her. Can't speak. My throat's dry, my chest is tight, but it's the shame that's choking me more than anything.

'What were you thinking?' she asks.

But I've already tuned out. Drifting in and out of whatever this groggy hell is. I'm awake, then asleep, then awake again. But I'm still fucking here.

And I don't know if I'm relieved or not?

Sarah came home early. Don't know why, maybe she had a gut feeling, maybe something just didn't sit right. Either way, she walked through that door and saved my life. I should be dead right now, but I'm not. Maybe that means something . . . maybe it's not my time. Maybe I'm meant to stay and fight this thing that's been eating away at me.

Kyle knows nothing. We've kept it quiet. As far as he's concerned, Dad just got a bad dose of the flu and needs a few days in bed. He pops his head in now and then; tells me he loves me and goes back to playing his games. And I just lie here, heart cracked open, thinking how close I came to leaving him for good.

What the fuck was I thinking?

The thought of him growing up without a dad . . . thinking I didn't love him enough to stay . . . it guts me. I can't believe I was ready to put that weight on his shoulders. I was supposed to protect him. Not become the ghost that haunts his childhood.

It's been a couple of months since I tried to end it all. Hard to even write that, let alone accept it. I've started therapy now, here in Edinburgh, private NHS clinic. Never thought I'd be the one sitting on that couch, but here I am. The female doctor is really nice, though. Small build, South African accent, gentle voice. There's a calmness about her, no judgment, just kindness. I actually feel like I can speak, properly speak, without the fear of being looked at like I'm broken.

She's given me some exercises to work on at home, little steps, but they feel like something. Just unloading some of the shit I've carried around for years . . . it's the first time I've felt maybe, just maybe, there's a bit of light breaking through this tunnel.

I'm working on things at home too, forcing myself out of the house, I'm training at the gym pretty consistently now. Sarah keeps asking me to go up with her to the stables, but I'm not really a horsey person and the thought of talking to her about things is too much. Kyle still knows nothing and he's going about his life as a normal child would. I spend more time with him, helping with homework and doing all the dad things I'm supposed to, taking him to school and his evening clubs, but I don't want to mix with the other parents. I just can't be bothered hearing about their problems.

Therapy's helping, though, slowly. Each session is giving me a little more clarity. My therapist reckons I'm carrying a mountain of guilt over what happened to Yves. 'Survivor's Guilt,' she called it. I always believed I could've done something, that maybe I should've gone in after him. The order to stand down haunted me for years, left me angry, bitter.

But she's helped me see it for what it really was. If I'd gone in, I'd be dead too. Simple as that. I didn't know the layout, the schematics, nothing. I would've driven straight into a kill zone, and there'd be eight more bodies added to the number.

August 2010

There's a nice big fella I've been chatting to at the gym for a few weeks, he's there most times I'm there and we've started training together regularly, proper graft, pushing each other hard, and for the first time in a while, I'm actually starting to feel a bit more like myself. We have a good laugh too, no heavy chat, no awkward questions. He only knows I did time in Iraq, nothing about the mess in my head, and I'm happy to keep it that way.

Turns out he runs a security company and runs the doors in a couple of clubs in town. He's asked me if I fancied working a couple of shifts a week for him. this could be something I need right now. A distraction. A way to slowly step back into the world again. I think I'll take him up on it.

I did door work on and off for years in between jobs and it was easy money, so I'm no stranger to it. He's also heavily into his martial arts, so we've started sparring. I trained martial arts my whole life but haven't done anything for a while, but being back in that rhythm, the sweat, the focus, the buzz, it's doing something for me. Feels like a part of me I thought I'd lost is waking back up.

I told Sarah about the weekend door work, and she seemed fine with it, didn't bat an eyelid really. I figured she would be. There's not much of a relationship left between us these days, not like we're some picture, perfect couple. If anything, I think she likes the idea of me being out the house, less chance she has to make small talk or pretend to like me. Truth is, it gives me something to do too. Better than sitting on the couch night after night, staring at the shite on telly while she disappears off to bed by 8pm.

Chapter 15

Rebuilding

After months of darkness, I didn't expect to laugh again. But then I met Callum . . .

The door work is a good distraction just now and I quite like the banter; I'm working with a big gym bunny called Callum, Bodybuilder with the biggest arms I've ever seen, Tanned, tattooed, and rocking a Viking beard even Odin would envy. We're working this fancy cocktail bar, the people are nice, an older crowd and civilised unlike some of the clubs I worked in the past.

I was working last weekend, and Callum and I are in deep conversation about bench pressing and the usual bloke chat, when a group of girls walked in. Honestly, I don't usually pay much attention, just do the usual nod, polite smile, and open the door, but this one girl, stunning shy-looking blonde . . . fuck me. We locked eyes as I said good evening and she gave me a smile as she walked past, and something hit me. Proper bolt of lightning shit. I turned to Callum and said, dead serious, 'She's going to be my wife.'

He laughed, 'Bollocks, you're married!'

'Yeah . . . But only on paper.'

I don't know what it was, maybe the way she looked at me, maybe the way the noise in the room just dropped away for a second, but I swear, it felt like I already knew her. Like some part of me had been waiting for her to show up. Callum's laughing away at me saying, 'You're dreaming Scotty boy, here, have a protein bar.'

I couldn't help myself, I know I'm married, but I've honestly never been blown away like this, I shouldn't even think it but can't help myself. I need to speak to her, just even to let her know . . .

Time keeps moving but half the time I feel stuck. Working weekends with Callum, I'll be laughing one minute and then bang, I'm back in the sandpit. My moods swing like a hammer. Some days I'm level, other days the anger rips straight through. I wrestle it down, but it's always there, waiting. The meds dull it, the counselling helps, but neither can kill it completely.

At home with Sarah and Kyle, the weight's heavier. Frustration eats away at me. I want to go back to Iraq, but my head's still a mess. The future feels like a fight I can't plan for.

Calls from the lads don't make it easier. They're all in the same hole, trying to claw their way out. We talk, reassure each other, pretend we've got it handled. Then the phone rings at 2am your mate on the line, voice shaking, ready to end it all. That's when it smashes into you, the war never finished. It just followed us home.

Last night, Callum and I were working the door when guess who walks in . . . the same girl from a few weeks back. This time just her and a pal. I looked at Callum and said, 'Fuck me, brother. Is this fate or what?' He didn't even blink, just shook his head and said, 'Be careful, mate.'

I wasn't going to let it slide again. I followed her in and walked straight up to the bar beside her. 'Hi again,' I said. She turned, smiled, same smile that stuck with me since the first time, and said, 'Hi again too.'

I nodded to the barman and told him I'd cover their drinks. She gently placed her hand on mine. 'Thank you, that's very kind.' That one little touch felt like someone had turned the lights back on.

I introduced myself properly, and she said her name was Kelly. Bit of small talk, nothing forced. Just . . . easy. Like we already knew each other, even though we'd only just met. She gave me her telephone number, but just after that, her eyes dropped to my hand. She clocked the ring.

'Oh . . . you're married.'

Bollocks. That's that fucked.

'It's complicated,' I said, trying to keep it light, but I knew the mood had shifted. She gave me a polite smile and said, 'Well, thanks for the drinks,' before walking back over to her table. 'It's best you don't call' she said.

And I just stood there, watching her go, feeling like the ground had dropped an inch beneath me.

I know I shouldn't be feeling like this. I'm married. But it's not a marriage it's just two people living under the same roof, no connection, no spark, nothing. The war has turned me into someone I can't stand, and it's obvious Sarah can't stand this version either.

And now this . . . this woman, this moment . . . it's stuck in my head. I can't shift it.

For the first time in years, I feel something real. A flicker of hope. A chance at happiness. I know what I have to do. I need to get out, to be honest, to stop pretending.

Because staying where I am, that's not living.

Is there a chance I could be happy again? I'm thinking, driving home from work. The roads are quiet, but my heads loud.

What about Kyle? Will he hate me? Will I fuck his life up for good? The guilt eats at me, then swings straight back to the mess in my own head.

Do I even deserve another shot at happiness? Is that selfish? Am I just dragging all this baggage into someone else's life?

It's doing my head in. One minute I'm dreaming of something new, of finally feeling alive again, starting new somewhere else, and the next I'm sinking. Fast. The darkness is creeping back in. That familiar knot of anger and frustration winding tighter in my chest.

I grip the steering wheel tighter, staring ahead, but I'm not really seeing the road. Just caught somewhere between a life I can't keep living and a future I'm terrified to step into.

5 November 2010 – 2100hrs

Guy Fawkes night. War disguised as celebration. I've got the TV volume cranked up just to drown out the fireworks outside, but it's useless. I'm sitting there, soaked in sweat, staring blankly at the screen like it's going to save me. Sarah's already in bed. Kyle's upstairs doing his usual, headphones in, oblivious.

They've no idea. No clue what's going on inside me.

Each explosion outside rips through my chest like I'm back in the shit. Baghdad. Fallujah. Basra. I swear I can hear the crack of AKs, sharp and close. My hands are clawed into the couch, gripping tight enough to make my fingers ache. Sweat's running down my back, cold and steady. My heart's thumping like it wants out.

Then comes her voice. Sarah. 'Turn the TV down, I'm trying to sleep.'

That's it. That's the fucking tipping point.

The noise outside, the war in my head, it's all too much. I cover my ears with my hands, trying to shut it all out. I'm rocking like a broken kid, eyes screwed shut. But I can't stop it, every shot fired, every face I can't forget, every bit of guilt I've tried to bury. It all hits at once.

And I snap – *'FUCK OFF, just, FUCK OFF!*

I don't even know who I'm shouting at anymore. The past? Myself? The world?

All I know is I'm still fighting. And right now, I'm fucking losing.

Sarah comes down. I hear her footsteps first, then her voice, softer this time. 'What's going on? Are you OK?'

Something's shifted. Like she's just now seen me properly for the first time in years. Maybe she's finally found her heart.

She leans over and holds me. No questions, no judgement. Just wraps her arms round me tight. I don't push it away. I let it happen.

She doesn't say a word. She just knows. She can feel it. The war in me. The fear. The shame. The fucking mess I've become.

She's rocking me like I'm a broken kid, and I'm nearly 40 years old, but it's comforting. It's what I need. That human touch. That closeness.

It doesn't fix everything, but it takes the edge off. Just enough.

I get up, head to the cupboard, grab the sleeping tablets and diazepam. Neck a couple without thinking. I just need sleep. Need this night to end.

This is shit.

Not that long ago I was a warrior. Head high, keeping my team alive, switched on and at the top of my game. Now I'm just trying to control my life falling apart.

A few days have passed since the fireworks, and surprise, Sarah's back to her usual self. Snapping at me for daft wee things. The washing, the way I made the bed, leaving a light on. Like none of last week happened.

What happened to that woman who held me when I was breaking? Do I really need to be on my knees, shaking and broken, before she shows a shred of compassion?

I sat there this morning, just staring into my coffee, and it hit me. Properly hit me.

It's over between us.

I've been clinging to this thing, hoping things would change. Hoping *she* would change. That maybe, just maybe, there was still something left between us. But I see it now, clear as day. There's nothing. Just two strangers living separate lives

I need out.

Because if I stay, I'll vanish completely. I need to feel something again. I need to be seen. To be understood. I can't spend the next 20 years walking on eggshells, stuck in this limbo, wondering *what if*.

Kyle . . . he's young. Yeah, it'll hurt, but he'll be alright. Look around any school nowadays, half the kids are from split homes. He'll adapt. And I'll make damn sure he knows I'm always there.

But me? I'm done living a lie.

This is the moment. The switch. The breakthrough.

I've survived war zones. I can survive this too.

It's time to go.

November 2011

I was plucking up the courage to speak to Sarah today, when my old pal called me and asked if I was working at the moment, I said not anything permanent, just doing a bit of door work, *not going into why of course*. He asked if I could do a job for a couple of weeks in Lithuania?

Absolutely mate, get me the fuck out of here! What's the job?

'I can't discuss over the phone, but I'll get the boss to call you'.

An hour later the call came in, a female on the other end . . . 'I've emailed you the paperwork to complete, once that comes in, you'll get a call back'.

A bit cloak and dagger, just tell me what the job is?

The phone rings, there's a guy on the phone this time, as usual a bit of a posh London voice 'Ok Scott, welcome on board, we have your paperwork, I'm emailing you the flight details, you will be briefed on the job once you land.'

This is doing my head in. There's comsec (Communication security) and then there's this? A bit over the top? Is this job even legal?

Sarah is not saying too much, 'do what you like' is her answer to most things, so I'm off!

Chapter 16

Back on OPs

Monday 29 November 2011

Saying goodbye again, but not like before. No drama this time, no drawn, out hugs or tears. Even Kyle wasn't that fussed. Guess two weeks in the arse-end of the former Soviet Union doesn't quite carry the same emotional weight as months in Iraq or Afghanistan. Fair enough. I was just glad to be getting back on the horse.

Flights were smooth. Edinburgh to London, then on to Vilnius. Coming through customs, I clock a guy holding a sign: *Mr. White*. Nothing else. Towering lad around 6ft 6, stone-faced, jeans and an old-fashioned leather blazer, an odd look but I guess it may be the trend here? He gives a slight nod and a sly grin when I walk up. To him 'Come,' he says, 'I'm Dmitri', he shakes my hand with this huge gorilla-sized mit! No talking, just straight out into the car park.

We get into this Black SAAB, nice motor but I've no idea where it's taking me, hopefully, a hotel and not the boot of a Lada with a shovel and plastic sheeting. Luckily, it's the former. I pull up at a hotel and spot a few other blokes hanging about in the lobby, same look I've got. Tired, confused, mildly suspicious. Then this English guy strolls in like he's late for a dinner party, big grin on his face, 'Hi lads, I'm David.'

There's six of us – four Brits, two Russians, including big Dmitri. David hands each of us an old burner phone and an envelope with a hotel name and address on it. 'You're all staying at separate places,' he says, cheerful as ever. 'Meet tonight at 2100hrs, room 21, Novotel city centre. We'll give you the brief then.'

Right. Because that doesn't sound shady as fuck.

Sitting there, staring at this cheap phone and a random hotel address, I just thought – *What the fuck have I walked into this time?* Honestly, felt like the start of some low-budget spy flick where the hero dies in the first five minutes.

Finally, I'm in the RV Hotel, in room 21 as asked, David then relaxes and offers us all brew.

We all introduce ourselves, our background and get to know each other a bit. I'm the only one here that's done Iraq / Afghanistan, the rest are ex-cops, and Circuit blokes from London.

David finally tells us the mission . . .

There is a bank here called the Snoros, it's going under, bankrupt, pardon the pun. Was being run by a Russian oligarch. However, the owner was spending more than what was coming in and ended up owing a lot of money to other dangerous people.

The CEO had fled the country but left some of his staff here to clean up before the government closes things down for good.

The task was a bit of an odd one. We were the close protection and counter-surveillance team, but the twist was, the principals weren't supposed to know we were there. Basically, we were running covert overwatch while they carried on blissfully unaware. Quiet work, but important. And truth be told, I was glad to be back in a job I loved.

There were three of them still involved with the bank, two men and a woman. We got handed their files, photos, personal details, the usual background stuff. The plan was to split the coverage so each of them had round, the, clock eyes on them.

I asked about weapons. We were told pistols were available if we really needed them, but the local weapons regs were tight. If we got caught carrying, it could land us in a mess. I pointed out the obvious how are we meant to protect someone if we can't fight back? The answer was what I expected: we'd stash a few strategically in the vehicles, just in case things went sideways. Not ideal, but it was something.

I was teamed up with a bloke called Jim. Ex-Special Branch, switched on and easy to work with. Before the job kicked off, I suggested we run our own recces, get familiar with the routes, mark, up hospitals and safe houses, put our own plan together instead of relying on someone else's. We spent a couple of days grafting, and the other lads chipped in with their own prep. Between us, we had the ground covered.

Now we're set. First shift starts tomorrow. Back on the tools, back doing what I was built for. This one's going to be interesting.

First shift, Lithuania in late November isn't exactly tropical, dark by four in the afternoon, air so cold it cuts through your jacket like a blade. Streets look clean enough, but there's this undercurrent, like everyone's watching everyone. You don't know if the guy smoking on the corner is just freezing his balls off or clocking your movements.

Jim and I are chatting. This is more his thing. I am more comfortable with the CP side of things, but Jim is an old hand at this.

We were tasked with the woman, Elena. Mid-thirties, smart dresser, serious face. She worked out of a grey Soviet-style office block, the kind of place that looked like a set from a Cold War film. We set up in an old car, nothing too flash, just another battered Volvo blending into the background.

The job should've been boring. Watch her go in, watch her come out, tail her discreetly, make sure nobody else is taking an interest. But around mid-morning we picked up something. A black BMW parked opposite, engine off, two guys inside. Locals, shaved heads, leather jackets, the uniform here. At first, could've been nothing. But then Elena leaves the building, and like clockwork, their eyes follow her.

Jim mutters, 'Well, that's not exactly subtle.'

I nod. 'You thinking what I'm thinking?'

He smirks. 'That we're not the only ones running surveillance here? Yeah.'

We let her go about her day, ducking in and out of cafés, meeting a couple of suits, nothing major. But the Beemer shadowed her at every stop, always just far enough back to play it cool.

That night, back at the Novotel, the mood was different. Not everyone had picked up tails, just seems to be us. Whoever was watching her, were organised. Not just a couple of local gangsters winging it.

David didn't seem rattled, but his grin was thinner than before. 'Gentlemen, this is precisely why you're here. We don't exactly know what these people want, but you're here to Keep them breathing, keep them un-spooked. That's your job.'

Easier said than done.

Day three, things escalated. Elena left work late, headed down into an underground car park. The Beemer followed, but this time only one of the blokes got out, hands stuffed in his jacket. Jim clocked it immediately. 'That's not a cigarette break.'

I didn't even think. Out of the Volvo, down the ramp, moving quick but casual. The bloke reached into his coat just as Elena fumbled for her keys. He stopped when he clocked me striding in, eyes like steel. Jim circled from the other side.

The guy weighed it up, then backed off, smiling and muttering something in Russian before disappearing into the stairwell.

Elena never noticed. She just drove out, blissfully unaware that she'd nearly been bagged in her own car park.

Back at the hotel, I couldn't shake it. Jim and I both agreed ,whoever these lads were, they were rehearsing. Measuring responses. Seeing how close they could get before someone stopped them.

And if that was the rehearsal . . . what the fuck was coming next?

We all take turns watching the residence and their movements; to be fair, it's easy money and I'm not worried. To be honest I don't think the threat is as high as we expected, think there's games being played but I can't imagine anyone is going to kill a women who works in a dodgy bank.

1900hrs

Jim and I are on Elena again, low key. She's out with some work pals tonight, tucked away in this quiet wee restaurant off the main drag. Quaint place. Too quiet for my liking. Would've been happier with a busy place where you blend in easier.

Jim and I take a table near the entrance – standard placement, eyes on the door. Elena and her lot are deeper inside, tucked into a corner booth. We order coffee, a light snack, pretend to talk, and wait it out.

Dinner goes smooth. No drama. They wrap up and start filtering out one by one. Jim and I get moving, eyes locked on Elena. We're mainly focused on her tonight. She heads out, but instead of going to her car – opposite direction – she turns and starts walking into a nearby park. Pitch black in there apart from the street lighting around it.

I glance at Jim, he's already peeled off to get the car. I radio him. 'I'll stay on her. You circle round. Keep it close.'

Only problem, I'm absolutely bursting for a piss. Held it in through the whole meal trying to stay sharp, and now it's a bloody emergency. I scan for a tree, but if I stop and she's grabbed or jumps in a car, I'm fucked. Either I piss myself or take my chances behind a bush.

Sod it, I need to go. if anyone could see me, Hoodie up, standing behind a bush with a face of ecstasy emptying my bladder pissing like a fucking racehorse.

Right, still tracking her, keeping just enough distance. She's walking with purpose now. Then I clock a black motor up ahead – half in shadow, engine running.

Wait a fucking second . . . I know that car. That's the same one that was tailing her a few days back.

Elena doesn't hesitate walks straight up to it. Bloke gets out, the same guy we clocked before. Big grin on his face like he's just won the lottery. She walks right into him, arms round his neck, then bang, full-on kiss.

I key the radio.

'Jim, you getting this?

'Certainly am,' he says, voice low. 'What the fuck . . .'

So much for the threat.

They jump in the car and drive off. I glance at Jim.

'Shall we tail them?'

'No point,' he says flatly. 'She's not in any danger.'

Fair enough.

We head back to the hotel, still trying to process what the hell we just saw. Sit down with the boss and give him the rundown. He just laughs, shakes his head.

'You couldn't make this shit up.'

He's not wrong.

Whatever's going on with Elena, it's way above my pay grade. We were hired to keep her safe, not untangle whatever mess she's mixed, up in. David pulls the plug on the job, says he's taking it upstairs. Tells his boss straight, it's an impossible task. Too many shadows, too many questions. And it's clear now... this is something much bigger than we were ever told.

We all head out that evening into town, get a few drinks and let our hair down. That was a bad idea, after a few too many vodkas I'm back in the hotel room head spinning, I'm frustrated, angry, the demons are back. The mini bar is getting smashed, time to sleep before heading back home tomorrow.

December

Sarah and I are at each other's throats most days now. I know I'm a pain in the arse to live with. It's the PTSD – doesn't excuse it, but it's there, always ticking in the background.

I've sent the odd message to Kelly, nothing heavy, just small talk. Didn't expect her to reply, but she did. She listens. Doesn't try to fix me, doesn't flinch. Just takes me as I am. That'll do for now. She's got a good heart, and I don't have to wear the mask with her.

I've just come in from the gym, Sarah's standing there, holding a bit of paper, anger and smug satisfaction written all over her face 'I checked your phone records,' she says, holding it out like evidence in a courtroom. 'You've been texting someone. Want to tell me who she is?' She throws it at me.

I don't even flinch. 'I can't lie to you, Sarah, I've been speaking to someone. But come on, we both know this was over for a long time. We're not the same people as we were before I went to Iraq. I came back broken, angry, numb, all of it. Kyle barely says two words to me now, and you spend more time with those bloody horses than you do in this house.'

Tears come on cue, but her eyes betray her. It's not heartbreak, it's relief

I'm standing there, dead behind the eyes. Nothing. The meds have stripped any feeling clean out of me. No anger, no guilt, just silence.

Sarah is now full of hatred, her lips tight as she says 'You better tell your son when he gets home,' 'You've ruined everything. You tell him this is all your fault, then get the fuck out.'

And just like that, it's real. No more pretending. No more holding it together for the sake of it.

What the fuck am I going to do now? What's Kyle going to say? Where do I even go? The cash is nearly gone, no chance of a hotel.

I drift round the house like a ghost. Sarah's locked herself in her bedroom. I sit there, waiting on the front door to open, this crushing weight in my gut. Shame, maybe. Regret? I don't even know anymore.

All I do know is . . . this is torture.

A few hours pass….

The front door creaks open.

Kyle steps in, hoodie up, headphones on, backpack sliding off his shoulder. Just another school day.

For a split second, I forget what's about to happen. Then I hear Sarah's footsteps pounding down the stairs like a warning bell.

I'm already sitting on the edge of the armchair in the living room, knees bouncing, palms sweaty, heart hammering against my ribs like it's trying to escape. My mouth's dry, throat closing in.

Sarah storms in and without even looking at me says, 'Kyle, come in here. Sit down next to me.'

He frowns, pulls his headphones down. 'Why? What's going on?'

Her voice is sharp and angry. 'Your dad's got something to tell you.'

Then she turns to me, eyes sharp. 'Go on. Tell him.'

He looks at me 'What's wrong', eyes already full of worry. My throat tightens. I can't swallow. Can't breathe.

'Mum and I…' I force the words out, barely a whisper. 'We can't live together anymore, son. I'm leaving.'

The room falls silent.

Kyle just stares at me, blinks once, like his brain's refusing to make sense of what he's just heard. Then it hits. Like a tsunami.

His face crumples, and the first sob bursts out of him like a gut punch.

'No . . . no. . . . no!'

He covers his face with both hands, the kind of cry that comes from deep inside, the kind you can't fake or control. His whole body starts to shake.. It's raw and broken and full of disbelief.

Sarah pulls him into her arms, rocking him like he's five again, and she glares at me like I've just shot him.

And the thing is, I feel like I have.

I stand up, move toward him, hand out like some pathetic gesture will fix this. 'Kyle, son . . . I'm sorry . . . I didn't mean . . .'

But he's gone. Rips himself out of her arms, sprints up the stairs two at a time. His bedroom door slams with a bang that echoes right through my chest.

Sarah turns on me. 'See what you've done?' she hisses. 'You've destroyed him. You piece of shit.'

I don't answer. What can I say? She's right.

I grab a bag, put together a couple of essentials, toothbrush, spare set of clothes, and my car keys.

I walk out into the freezing evening air, the sky heavy and black, like the night is grieving with me. The door clicks shut behind me, and I just stand there.

My boy. My world.

He looked at me like I was a stranger. Like he hated me.

And the worst part is . . . I deserve it.

I drive around aimlessly; streets I've known all my life now blurred through tears. I don't know where I'm going, just know I can't go back.

Then I pull over and stare at my phone. One name – Mum.

We've not spoken properly in months, not since the last row. I feel pathetic even thinking of calling her. But I've got nothing left. I hit dial. It rings once.

'Hiya, son, how are you?'

My voice cracks.

'Not good, Mum. Can I come over?'

Pause.

'Aye, of course. Everything okay?'

I swallow hard.

'I'll explain when I get there.'

Chapter 17

Still Standing

November 2021

Not every story ends the way you once hoped, but mine came close. Close enough to feel proud of. Close enough to know I made it through and built something solid on the other side.

I used to think there'd be a moment, some kind of turning point. A line in the sand where I could say, 'That's where it all ended . . . and that's where the healing began.' But life's not like that. It doesn't hand you closure. It leaves you with quiet gaps, unanswered questions, and the kind of scars no one else can see.

The truth is, my son and I never got through this battle, and we don't speak anymore.

A lifetime of missed calls, misunderstood silences, and things said that can't be unsaid or forgotten. Maybe one day he'll pick up the phone. Maybe one day I will. But right now, there's a gap between us that neither of us has the strength, or the words, to cross. That's a wound we both can't heal.

I still think of him, wonder if he's alright. Wonder what kind of man he's becoming. If he ever wonders about me. I'll always carry that, tucked away.

But even so, life found a way forward.

Kelly and I finally met up and we ended up together, she was my saviour. Gentle. Real. She didn't ask questions I couldn't answer. Didn't push or prod at the cracks. She just accepted me. As I was. As I am. She stood by me when most people would've turned away. She saw something in me I couldn't even see myself.

We married within three years. Not as a fix, but through love, honesty and trust, something I never thought was possible. A commitment to each other's storms. With her, I found a stillness I hadn't known in years. And in that stillness, after the noise of Iraq, after the chaos of coming home, I found something I thought I'd lost for good: Real Love and Peace.

It wasn't easy. It still isn't. There are mornings I wake up with a heavy heart after a dream. Days when the weight of everything I've seen, everything I've done, crushes the breath out of me. But now… but the therapy helped get me back on my feet again and with Kelly, I'm not doing it alone. That makes all the difference.

And I found purpose again.

Not as a soldier, or a contractor, but here, on home soil. I joined the fire service.

It's a different kind of war. A different kind of chaos. One where the enemy is time, smoke, heat. Where lives are on the line, but your job is to save them. It gave me a new team. A new sense of duty. A reason to show up.

Some of the lads know bits of my past. Some don't. But it doesn't matter. What matters is the job. The camaraderie. The feeling that what we do still counts for something. I swapped the rifle for a hose reel, the convoy for the fire engine, and I haven't looked back.

I still have the odd rough day. Flashbacks. Triggers. Nights where I lie awake, reflecting on my life, my memories. But I don't live there anymore. I don't drown in it. I'm living again.

And if you've carried your own war, whether it was in uniform or in silence, whether it happened thousands of miles away or in your own home, then I hope my story has shown you something important:

You are not broken. You are not alone.

I'll never be the same man I was before it all started. But I've made peace with that. I'm still here. Still standing. Still moving forward. You can be too.